Navigating through the Cloud

A plain English guide to surviving the risks, costs and governance pitfalls of Cloud computing

Rob Livingstone

Disclaimer

Every effort has been made to ensure that *Navigating through the Cloud* is as accurate as possible. However, typographical and/or content errors may exist and this book should only be used as a guide.

This book is distributed and/or sold with the express understanding that the contents of this book do not constitute commercial, technical, regulatory and/or legal advice and are based solely upon the author's personal and professional experience and/or research and is believed to be accurate and reliable at the time of publication. It is the reader's full responsibility to assess the veracity, applicability and validity of any facts, opinions, ideas and suggestions contained in this book, whether suggested or implied for themselves.

Specific questions regarding international jurisdictional law, commercial law, tort law, intellectual property law, copyright law, patent and/or trademark law should be addressed to competent members of those professional areas.

The purpose of *Navigating through the Cloud* is to provide a broad understanding of Cloud Computing in the context of Software as a Service (SaaS) within organisations . The author and/or publisher shall have neither liability nor responsibility to any person or entity with respect to any loss or damage caused, or alleged to be caused, directly or indirectly whatsoever by the information contained in this book.

The scanning, uploading, and distribution of this book via the Internet or by any other means without the permission of the author is illegal and punishable by law. Please purchase only authorized printed or electronic editions and do not participate in or encourage electronic piracy of copyrighted materials. We appreciate your support of the author's rights.

———

Artwork by Attactivo. www.attractivo.com.au

Livingstone, Robin P., 1956-
Navigating through the Cloud / Rob Livingstone – 1st Ed.

ISBN-13: 978-1461152859 Pbk.
ISBN-10: 1461152852 Pbk.

Navigating through the Cloud

A plain English guide to surviving the risks, costs and governance pitfalls of Cloud computing

* * *

"A clear, business-oriented, non-technical book that enables CEOs to understand Cloud and make an objective and well-informed assessment of its relevance and value to their business."

- James O'Toole
Joint Managing Director, CEO Forum Group, Australia

"Illuminating both its advantages and drawbacks, Livingstone wields a sharp knife of experience and clear thinking to cut through the thick clouds of hype enveloping Cloud computing today, asking the critical questions businesses both large and small should (and all too often don't) ask about Cloud adoption."

- David Rosenbaum
Senior editor, technology, CFO Magazine and cfo.com, Boston, USA

"This professionally written book clearly explains, in terms relevant to all organisations, the implications and challenges that managers will face in implementing enterprise Cloud computing. Based on rich experience in a broad range of business contexts, this is a book that every business leader should read."

- **Professor Ken Dovey**
  Director: Information Technology Management
  Program, University of Technology, Sydney, Australia.

"A must-read for any executive trying to differentiate Cloud hype from reality. Using real world language, it provides the reader with the knowledge to ask the right questions to determine risk versus business value and innovation".

- **Caroline Bucknell**
  General Manager, CIO Executive Council, Australia

"A practical, no-nonsense guide for business executives at all levels."

- **Georgina Swan**
  Editor: CIO Magazine, Australia.

* * *

To Cathie, Douglas, Natasha and Robert

* * *

Table of Contents

Preface   xiii

Chapter Outline   xxi

1: Cloud Technology – What is it and why should I care?   1

What is Cloud computing?   3

What are the key elements of Cloud computing?   4

Why is this book focussing primarily on
Software as a Service (SaaS)?   6

Cloud at the peak of the Gartner™ 'Hype-Cycle' –
What does this mean?   6

Why is this Cloud 'Hype-Cycle' different?   8

Is Cloud just another form of outsourcing?   9

Why is Cloud so potentially compelling?   10

How do Public vs. Private Cloud offerings differ?   13

Public Cloud: What is meant by a 'multi-tenanted'
system?   13

What about the risks in Public Cloud?   14

Which executive is accountable for Cloud
systems in your organisation?   15

The takeaway messages from this chapter are: 16

2: The democratisation or consumerisation of IT   17

The conventional 'on-premises' IT system
Cloud: Implement now, modify later   18
Cloud computing: Making changes by
configuration, not programming   19
Public Cloud: Good for individuals and
organisations alike?   20
Cloud and the changing role of IT   21
Is Cloud driving the transformation of the enterprise
IT department?   22
What are the implications for procurement?   23
The takeaway messages from this chapter are: 26

3: Cloud: Inversion of the IT business case? - '*buy* before
you try'   27

On-premises enterprise systems: The *buy-and-
depreciate* approach   27
Cloud enterprise systems: The '*buy before you try'*
business model   28
Impact of adding integration to other systems   29
Managing runaway complexity   31
How will Cloud help innovation?   32
The takeaway messages from this chapter are: 33

4: A field guide to the management of Cloud vendors   35

The emphasis is on the 'product demonstration'   36

Pet-shop marketing: Take the puppy home for the
weekend   36
'Top-down' sales strategy: Driving the wedge between
IT and the business   37
The role of your IT department in dealing with vendors 38
The takeaway messages from this chapter are: 40

5: Cloud vendor contract and legal considerations   41

Understand your Cloud vendor's contract   41
Contract duration   42
Request a copy of the draft contract as early as
possible   43
in the sales process
What form does the contract take?   44
The 'I accept' logon checkbox   44
Contract variations   44
Considerations for multinational corporations   45
Other contract considerations   45
The takeaway messages from this chapter are: 50

6: Opinions… Opinions…. Who do I trust?   51

'Cloud-huggers' and 'tin-huggers'   51
Cloud is a technology and delivery mechanism
choice, not a philosophy!   52
The ultimate proof: Proof of concept trail   52
The role of consultants: pre-sale, selection and
implementation   53
Key attributes to look for in Cloud consultants: 54

The takeaway messages from this chapter are: 57

7: Low cost - 'Like a sub-prime mortgage?' 59

Importance of the approach to licensing models 60
Comparing costs between Cloud and on-premises:
The two questions 64
Cost certainty over the lifespan of the Cloud system 71
Third party Cloud providers 72
Unrestricted or enterprise Cloud offerings – Good value? 73
Switching to the Cloud: Cheap and easy? 73
Likely to change usage patterns in the future? 74
Summary 74
The takeaway messages from this chapter are: 75

8: Risk – the gorilla in the dark room? 77

Risk: The obvious questions 77
Risk: The less obvious questions 79
Other factors influencing risk. 81
The takeaway messages from this chapter are: 84

9: The problem of today = the solution and opportunity
of tomorrow 85

Speed and the evolution of Cloud computing 85
The penalties of switching Cloud vendors 87
Utility computing and the electricity grid analogy:
Partly true? 88
Time will heal the wounds of early adopters 90
The takeaway messages from this chapter are: 91

10: Implications for multinational and transnational
corporations   93

    The takeaway messages from this chapter are: 97

11: Suitability for Cloud: What's your business environment?
How proprietary are your current systems?   99

    What is the likely life expectancy of the system?   103
    Lack of finance   104
    Uncertainty over the number of system users over time   104
    The takeaway messages from this chapter are: 106

12: Implications for governance   107

    What are the key governance questions you need to ask?   108
    What are some of the project management issues
in Cloud computing?   109
    The takeaway messages from this chapter are: 112

13: The promise of the imminent future   113

    Cloud facilitating innovation   113
    Cloud for the desktop   114
    Stick to the fundamentals   115

14: The Cloud Assessment Framework   117

    You know the upside with precision. What about
the possible downsides?   117

The Cloud Assessment Framework – just a suggestion   118
Request for Tender (RFT) / Request for Quote (RFQ)   119
How to use the Framework   120

The Questions: 127

1. Architecture and solution fit   127
2. Audit   127
3. Change Control   128
4. Consulting   130
5. Contract end   131
6. Cost   133
7. Drivers   137
8. Governance   140
9. Implementation   144
10. Innovation   146
11. Integration   147
12. IT Staff   150
13. Contracts   151
14. Legislation   153
15. Multinational   154
16. Procurement   156
17. Risk & Security   158
18. Service Level Agreements + Penalties   162
19. Third Party Applications   163

Index   165

Preface

This book is a practical, plain English guide that discusses the commercial, governance, risk and cost issues of Cloud for *your* business, and provides you with an easy to understand framework to assess the cost and risk of moving to the Cloud.

This book is for executives and stakeholders in your organisation with a vested interest in the successful implementation of Cloud projects and the use of your organisation's IT systems.

It insightfully and professionally reveals the kinds of issues that you are likely to face in adopting Cloud technologies in your business.

Focus on Software as a Service (SaaS)

Also known as the *Public Cloud*, SaaS is sometimes referred to as "software on-demand". You pay for what you use through a regular subscription service, and the software is accessed over the Internet. Your own nothing, except the data you load into the system.

SaaS is where the majority of risk, complexity, cost and governance issues reside, and for this reason, it forms the focus of this book.

'Utility' Computing: Not the whole story

In his book "The Big Switch: Rewiring the World, From Edison to Google" (W.W. Norton, 2008), Nicholas Carr all but declared the pending death of IT. "In the long run, the IT department is unlikely to survive, at least in its familiar form," he writes. "IT will have little left to do once the bulk of business computing shifts out of private data centres and into 'the Cloud.'".

Business units and even individual employees will be able to control the processing of information directly, without the need for a bench full of technical specialists. This may be true in the very long term, but between now and then lie the fields that are littered with landmines for the ill informed and unwary.

Cloud technology is seen by many as the next disruptive IT innovation, essentially ushering in the era of 'utility' computing, analogous to utilities such as water and electricity. This hides the truth that, unlike truly utility based services, the cost, risk and effort of switching from one Cloud provider to another *is not trivial*. This is where the Cloud 'utility' computing and electricity grid analogy fails.

Opinions… opinions and more opinions….

There are an ever increasing number of industry analysts and 'Cloud evangelists' that see Cloud as being inevitable. Even if you are not currently considering Cloud, you will almost certainly be doing so at some point in the future.

Cloud computing is moving from early adolescence to maturity. This book is a timely field guide aiming to fill the gap in information that exists until the time that Cloud computing has fully matured in the market, and its value, risk, cost and relevance will be well understood by consumers, businesses, consultants and the IT industry alike.

Within the IT Industry, there are Cloud conferences, vendor breakfast events, 'Cloud specialists', self appointed and self proclaimed Cloud evangelists, and others who are clamouring to be heard above the Cloud 'noise'.

In the midst of this clamour, how can you make an objective and well-informed decision on whether Cloud is relevant and/or appropriate for *your* business, either now, or at some point in the future?

The appeal of Cloud computing

The primary appeal of Cloud can be summarised as:

- Cloud eliminates the need for on-premises IT infrastructure

- You pay for what you consume (known as the 'utility' computing model)

- The provider does the maintenance, operation and support of the system. You need not be involved in any of these aspects, reducing the need for you to employ expensive IT specialists

- Cloud potentially offers much faster IT projects, as software is all 'out the box' and can be launched in hours, if not minutes. This is in stark contrast to the relative slow speed of deploying on-premises IT systems that are managed by your conventional in-house IT department.

There are, however, some potentially serious risk and governance issues that exist in the Cloud for the unwary. In Cloud computing, not all risk is transferable, and it is important that you understand that, in principle:

- Responsibility can be outsourced, while

- Accountability cannot be outsourced.

Ultimately, it is your organisation's reputation at stake.

Size matters

Cloud is of immediate and significant value to consumers and small-medium sized organisations alike, as it grants immediate access to software systems that previously were only available to larger corporations, at a fraction of the cost and with minimal complexity and risk.

Mid-size to large organisations, however, face a number of challenges in the adoption of Public Cloud technologies.

The costs, risks and governance challenges rise significantly with organisational scale and complexity. This becomes even more relevant if you are a multinational or transnational organisation, which may cover multiple regulatory and statutory environments. Technical complexity, cost and governance are further increased if the Cloud system is to be interfaced to your on-premises systems.

This book focuses on the adoption of Cloud in mid-sized to larger organisations. Small enterprises with a high dependency on their IT systems should, nevertheless, still find this book useful, as some of the governance and risk issues discussed are still very applicable and relevant in these organisations.

Why did I write this book?

Essentially, I wrote a book that I could not buy.

Given my experience in the implementation and management of Public and Private Cloud technologies since 2005, I felt the need to 'download' my cumulative experience and knowledge into a book that allows individuals and organisations alike to make an objective and well-informed assessment of the value of Cloud.

- The real trigger was when I had transformed the entire IT cost of a national organisation to a *per user per month by application*, and was surprised to find that the 'low cost' Cloud system was in fact the *highest cost per user* application out of all the applications used across the entire business, whether they be on-premises, hosted or Cloud.

There are a number of stressed Cloud projects emerging, which are, for obvious reasons, not being broadcast. These include:

- Recently, a nationwide Australian financial services organisation discovered to their detriment that 'hard-stop' performance limits inherent in the Cloud provider's environment prevented large parts of their application from being launched. This was only remedied by a redesign of the system, which resulted in the initial development budget being exceeded and the initial project schedule being delayed.

- In the absence of a clearly articulated and enforceable Cloud policy, a leading Australian University experienced an unauthorised deployment of a Cloud system that was funded from one Faculty's discretionary budget, as it fell within their prevailing local discretionary expenditure approval limits. This was only noticed when data integrity issues within their core student enrolments databases started occurring.

These outcomes would have been avoided should the appropriate due diligence and governance frameworks been in place at the start.

Ask the right question, get the right answer

Knowing what questions to ask, and of whom, will allow you to make a well informed decision on Cloud.

Think of this book as providing your executive team with a radar system with which to navigate your metaphorical aircraft around the mountains in the Cloud.

It is important that *you* assess *your* current Cloud plans against the information contained in this book. It could save you time, money, and in extreme cases, your business.

It is also important that organisations considering a move, or a further expansion, into Cloud computing do so from a fully informed basis, and make decision on the basis of evidence, not opinions or reliance on compelling vendor presentations alone!

Rob Livingstone
Sydney, Australia
July 2011

www.rob-livingstone.com

* * *

About the Author

Rob Livingstone is a respected and experienced CIO, with over 33 years of professional experience in the corporate world, the last 16 of which were as Oceania regional CIO in a number of multinationals.

Prior to entering the IT world as a CIO in the mid 90s, Rob held a number of senior operational, strategic advisory and executive positions in a range of industries both locally and overseas. These included defence-aerospace, manufacturing, public utility, packaging, construction through to logistics.

With a clear understanding of the financial, operational, risk, commercial and human factors that make a modern, complex business operate; Rob can triangulate these with his extensive knowledge of what value IT can bring to a business.

Rob has presented at a number of local and international conferences and industry events on topics such as collaboration, innovation, Cloud, unified communications and organisational productivity, as well as facilitated a number of industry workshops.

Being an active member of the CIO Executive Council, Rob has contributed to a number of events by holding workshops on topics such as Project Management and Cloud computing.

Rob is a well-rounded executive with extensive experience and deep knowledge on how companies can avoid the many pitfalls that lie in wait on the IT super-highway of unrealistic expectations and surprises!

Rob is the owner of Rob Livingstone Advisory Pty Ltd.

Chapter Outline

Chapter 1: Cloud Technology – What is it and why should I care?

This first chapter provides an introduction to Cloud computing and why it is important for you to understand basic Cloud computing concepts before committing your organisation to this technology.

Chapter 2: The democratisation or consumerisation of IT

This chapter explores a number of concepts behind the 'utility' computing model, and how this differs from the traditional on-premises model. In particular it discusses Cloud and the changing role of IT, implications for procurement, and how Cloud can facilitate the transformation of your IT department.

Chapter 3: Cloud: Inversion of the IT business case? - *'buy before you try'*

This chapter explores the differences in the selection of Cloud computing systems over conventional on-premises systems, as well as the risk of runaway complexity in Cloud implementations requiring multiple system-system interfaces. The role of Cloud in facilitating innovation is also discussed.

Chapter 4: A field guide to the management of Cloud vendors

The approach to selling Cloud systems differs somewhat to that of conventional on-premises IT systems in a number of ways. Understanding these sales approaches is important in being able to identify the strengths and weaknesses of the particular offer earlier in the sales cycle, thereby saving you time, effort, cost and potential surprises.

Chapter 5: Cloud vendor contract and legal considerations

This chapter details the important factors that should to be considered when negotiating your provider's contract. Unlike on-premises IT systems, you typically only have rights to retrieve only the data that you have loaded into the system. Also because Cloud is external to your organisation, it is an entity over which you have no control.

Chapter 6: Opinions... Opinions.... Who do I trust?

Currently, there is a wealth of opinion, misunderstanding, and some degree of opacity as to what Cloud is. This chapter explores how Cloud can be deployed and where the intrinsic value potentially lies. The concept of 'Cloud-huggers' and 'tin-huggers' is discussed, in the context of the sometimes polarised opinions held on Cloud. The importance of the Proof of Concept (POC) trial is also explained.

Chapter 7: Low cost - 'Like a sub-prime mortgage?'

A key tenet of Cloud computing is low cost, and this chapter expands on this crucial aspect to illustrate that this is not always the case. Moving from a capital purchase to a perpetual subscription model also presents a challenge to the unaware, in that the low initial cost may prove to be anything but that over a period of time.

Chapter 8: Risk – the gorilla in the dark room?

Entrusting your organisation's systems to 'someone out there on the Internet' is somewhat a step of faith for some organisations. This chapter explores ways of objectively and comprehensively assessing these risks.

Chapter 9: The problem of today = the solution and opportunity of tomorrow

This chapter explores the issues around the *Early adopter's advantage* vs. being a *Fast Follower*. As the technology and industry matures, the shortcomings of today will no doubt be progressively resolved. This chapter also explores the comparison between the Cloud 'Utility Computing' and the electricity grid analogy, and discusses where this analogy breaks down.

Chapter 10: Implications for multinational and transnational corporations

Cloud in the context of multinational or large multidivisional, transnational organisations is explored. Each business' environment is likely to differ on a country by country basis, as are their statutory and regulatory frameworks. The purpose of this chapter is to illustrate some of the possible scenario's that could arise.

Chapter 11: Suitability for Cloud: What's your business environment?

This chapter explores Cloud in the context of the nature and structure of your business, including its stage in the maturity cycle, its structure and your risk appetite.

Chapter 12: Implications for governance

Potentially, there are a range of statutory and regulatory frameworks that may apply to your organisation. These vary by country, legal jurisdiction, industry services and types of products sold. This chapter discusses the potential impacts that such frameworks may have, as well as exploring some implications for enterprise IT project management.

Chapter 13: The promise of the imminent future

This chapter explores how Cloud will continue to provide opportunities for increased productivity, value and flexibility, potentially at a lower Total Cost of Ownership (TCO). The role of Cloud in facilitating innovation and driving changes in the enterprise desktop PC environment is also discussed in this chapter.

Chapter 14: The Cloud Assessment Framework

The heart of the framework comprises a series of 'plain English' questions that need to be asked of all stakeholders, to ensure that all relevant aspects of cost, governance, risk and value are adequately discovered and summarised for scrutiny. A step-by-step process is also suggested, that will allow you to adapt this framework to *your* specific environment.

* * *

* * *

Chapter One

* * *

Cloud Technology – What is it and Why should I care?

Non-IT executives need to be aware, in broad terms, of Cloud computing, as it:

*   Is a potentially disruptive technology

*   Has the *potential* for your organisation to lower IT costs, and add value by having systems that are better designed and easier to use, whilst increasing IT departmental productivity, and

*   May expose your organisation to additional cost, technical, security and governance risks that are not normally associated with 'on-premises' IT systems and infrastructure.

Some possible scenarios include:

*   Your chosen Cloud solution offers a lower total cost of operation, however your Cloud provider may be unable to provide you with an effective escrow arrangement, due to the technical design of their infrastructure. Should the provider cease to exist, so do your systems. Period. Your business ceases trading

- Your Cloud system exists in a number of international legal jurisdictions, and may be subject to seizure or shutdown if the provider is in material breach of foreign legal and regulatory controls. This is totally out of your control

- Some Cloud solutions do not offer on-demand backup and immediate 'rollback' of your system in the event that a program interface upgrade fails. This could result in a number of issues, including either a non-compliance being flagged during your annual external audit on IT General controls, or present problems in a top-down SOX 404 risk assessment (Section 404 of the Sarbanes-Oxley Act of 2002).

This chapter outlines important aspects of Cloud computing by posing a series of questions that provides some insight into the Cloud computing model, namely:

1. What is Cloud computing?

2. What are the key elements of Cloud computing?

3. Why is this book focussing primarily on Software as a Service (SaaS)?

4. Cloud computing is at the peak of the Gartner™ 'Hype-Cycle' – What does this mean?

5. *Why* is this Cloud 'Hype-Cycle' different?

6. Is Cloud just another form of outsourcing?

7. Why is Cloud so potentially compelling?

8. How do Public vs. Private Cloud offerings differ?

9. Public Cloud: What is meant by a 'multi-tenanted' system?

10. What about the risks in Public Cloud?

11. Which executive is accountable for Cloud systems in your organisation?

Each question is explored in the following discussions.

What is Cloud computing?

Cloud is a very broad term for the 'IT systems accessed via the Internet'. The various components are all run by an external party, and you do not own anything, other than the *data* that you load into the system.

The primary attributes of Cloud systems are:

- You subscribe to the service on, typically, a *per user per month* basis (although you may pay annually *in advance*)

- The system is accessed via the Internet

- You neither have control or title over your Public Cloud provider's applications or IT infrastructure.

What are the key elements of Cloud computing?

Figure 1 illustrates the components of Cloud computing in broad terms.

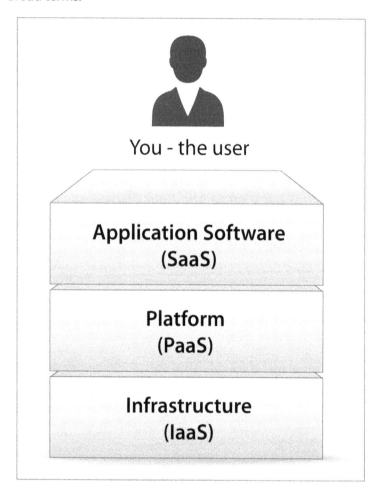

Figure 1: The key components of Cloud computing

Cloud computing has three primary elements, these being:

Software as a Service (SaaS)

- SaaS is what you use to run your business. One example of this is the Cloud Customer Relationship System (CRM), Salesforce™. Some organisations' entire sales processes depend on Salesforce™

- SaaS is sometimes referred to as "software on-demand". Ostensibly, you pay for what you use through a *subscription service*, and the software is accessed over the Internet. Your own nothing, except the data *you* load into the system.

Platform as a Service (PaaS)

- PaaS is transparent to the end user

- PaaS essentially, is the framework on which you can build software applications

- PaaS offerings facilitate the deployment of applications without the cost and complexity of buying and managing the underlying hardware and software yourself. Think of it as a form of renting part of a data centre.

Infrastructure as a Service (IaaS)

- IaaS is transparent to the end user

- IaaS delivers computer infrastructure - typically a platform virtualization environment - as a service. Think of this as 'the box', or server

- Virtualisation is a technology that permits many 'virtual' servers to run off a single physical server, as if they were separate machines. This maximises the capacity of the server and lowers unit cost. It allows the IaaS providers to share many clients on the same infrastructure, in a multi-tenanted structure

• The creation of virtual servers can be automated, and can take seconds or minutes rather than hours for the equivalent physical server. This underpins the inherent flexibility and 'on-demand' nature of Cloud computing.

Why is this book focussing primarily on Software as a Service (SaaS)?

You, your staff, your customers and others interact with your business systems at the *software layer* and it is this area that forms the focus of this book, as:

• SaaS is where the majority of risk, complexity, cost and governance issues reside

• SaaS defines your organisation's business system and business logic

• SaaS stands between the users and the underlying layers of server hardware, networks and data centre infrastructure layers of PaaS and IaaS. These platform and infrastructure layers are largely invisible to the end user, and are generally of little interest, provided the systems are stable and operate with acceptable performance.

Cloud at the peak of the Gartner™ 'Hype-Cycle' – What does this mean?

Gartner™, the worldwide US based information technology research and advisory organisation, coined the phrase 'Hype-Cycle' in the mid 90s to characterize the over-enthusiasm or "hype" and subsequent disappointment that often happens when organisations adopt new technologies.

The Gartner™ Hype-Cycle is highly relevant to Cloud computing. Cloud computing is currently at the peak of the Gartner™ Hype-Cycle, and is still predicted to be between two and five years from mainstream adoption.

Figure 2 illustrates the relationship between the various phases of the Hype-Cycle, these being:

Technology Trigger: The breakthrough, new technology or innovation that generates significant media and IT industry interest.

Peak of Inflated Expectations: A frenzy of publicity typically generates over-enthusiasm and unrealistic expectations.

Trough of Disillusionment: Technologies enter the "trough of disillusionment" because they fail to meet initial expectations and quickly become unfashionable. Consequently, the press usually shifts focus off the topic and the technology.

Slope of Enlightenment: Businesses (suppliers and customers alike) begin to really understand the benefits and where the technology is best applied.

Plateau of Productivity: The technology is well understood, mature and its benefits become well accepted.

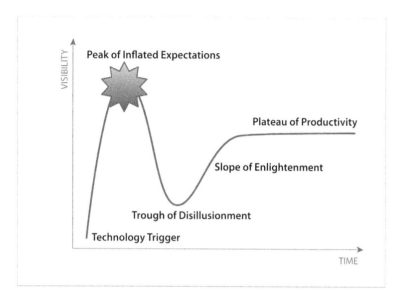

Figure 2: Cloud computing: Currently at the peak of the Gartner 'Hype-Cycle'

Why is this Cloud 'Hype-Cycle' different?

Over the years, there have been many previous 'Hype-Cycles', which largely were relevant to the IT industry, and were essentially directed to the IT Industry itself. The primary focus and appeal of these technologies was not the public at large or line-of-business managers and executives, but the IT industry itself.

- Some of these 'Hype-Cycles' included Client Server technology, ERP Systems, CRM system, eCommerce and Service Oriented Architecture (SOA), to name but a few.

Cloud, on the other hand is somewhat different, in that users and organisations are able to implement complex and powerful IT systems without any involvement from their IT department. There has also been broad acceptance of Cloud by individuals through the use of systems such as Gmail™, Facebook™ and YouTube™.

This difference can be summed up in two words:

- **Delivery** is possible without involvement from your IT department

- **Consumption** (i.e. use) of the Cloud system can be independent of any services or support from your IT department.

Cloud specifically is most appealing to the end user and non-IT management due to its ready access, ease of use, negligible entry cost, and apparent simplicity.

- Some Cloud vendors preferentially appeal directly to you, as non-IT executives and line-of-business managers. Chapter 4 provides an additional discussion on Cloud vendor sales strategies

- Vendors secure your initial interest and enthusiasm for Cloud computing by presenting graphically rich, flexible and compelling user interfaces to their systems, and in doing so, avoid having to address some of the difficult risk, cost and governance questions that are unlikely to be raised by this section of the user community.

Is Cloud just another form of outsourcing?

Cloud is analogous to outsourcing in that:

- An external party provides (software and infrastructure) services to your organisation

- A service and supply contract exists which contains minimum performance and service levels and penalties for non compliance to these minimum standards, and

- It is under a formal contractual arrangement.

However, some differences are:

- You cannot *readily* switch Cloud providers, as no common industry standards exist

- You may not be able to say with certainty *where* your data and programs are actually located

- You may have limited to no rights to step into a Cloud provider's infrastructure to claim your systems in the event of a contract termination, even if it were technically possible to do so

- The service provider's systems may cross multiple international legal jurisdictions

- You may not be entitled (or physically able to) retrieve *your* business logic vested in the SaaS system at the conclusion of the contract, although you can retrieve your data.

Why is Cloud so potentially compelling?

At face value, Cloud computing can appear to be a very compelling offer to non-IT executives and line of business managers. There are, however governance, cost and risk considerations that need to be aired and actively discussed within your organisation, to ensure that the complete picture is understood.

- In fact, there is a need for *greater* due diligence should your organisation seriously consider implementing Public Cloud, due to a combination of a range of factors such as potential opacity over the Total Cost of Ownership (TCO), product capability and technical limitations when combined with the volatility and speed of Cloud technology evolution.

After having explored all aspects, mitigated known risks and considered possible or likely costs, Cloud computing has the potential to:

- Lower IT operational cost

- Improve IT productivity by spending less time and effort in 'keeping the lights on'

- Drive value-added IT and business activities

- Foster innovation, due to the inherent flexibility of Cloud

- Speed up IT system deployments

- Offer a way of simplifying the complexities of enterprise IT, and

- Offer a way of putting IT systems in the hands of users – the 'democratisation of IT' effect.

The SaaS Cloud computing model is particularly attractive and compelling to some business executives, as:

It is available immediately…..

- Potentially, the system can be operational with only some minor configuration changes to suit your business in a very short timeframe – hours, days or weeks.

It allows you to '*Buy* before you try'……

- As the system can be delivered almost immediately, this allows your organisation to buy a few user subscriptions and try the system. If it does not meet your needs, the walk-away costs are negligible

- This is a fundamental shift in the value proposition for enterprise IT, in that an enterprise IT system can be implemented at the start, with minimal effort.

- Chapter 3 covers this in more detail.

It results from a compelling vendor offer......

- It is not uncommon for Cloud vendors to bypass the IT department and go directly to the non-IT executive levels of organisations with an ostensibly compelling offer. This may minimise the probability of factors such as lifecycle total cost, risk and governance being raised during this initial sales engagement process. The difficult questions may be relegated to a later date (provided you know what questions to ask, that is!)

- This has the effect of bypassing the CIO and the IT Department, in the attempt to generate a compelling need at the executive levels of organisations, ahead of an appropriate due diligence process.

- Chapter 4 covers this in more detail.

You already have had a positive personal experience with Cloud.....

- Personal experience in using Cloud applications (e.g. YouTube™, Linkedin™ Gmail™, etc…) are invariably positive due to their ease of use, low cost (if not free!), and/or

- There is a groundswell of opinion within your organisation favouring a Cloud offering as it avoids having to possibly deal with an internal IT department that may appear to be slow, inflexible or indifferent to Cloud.

How do Public vs. Private Cloud offerings differ?

Essentially, Public and Private Cloud are terms used to describe the physical location and ownership structures of the Cloud system.

- The **Public Cloud** is hosted on a service provider's infra-structure 'somewhere in the universe' and you own nothing, except your data that you upload. It is only accessible via the Internet. It could be located in different countries and jurisdictions. Well known Public Cloud providers include Salesforce™, Google™ and Amazon™

- A **Private Cloud** is owned by you, or your nominated ser-vice provider. In the latter case, you have the rights to access and manage the system under contract, as if it were yours. It may reside on your own premises, or on a data centre pro-vider of your choosing. You retain full control over the rel-evant components of the infrastructure, and therefore have full visibility over the design, operation and integrity of the system. You can walk into your provider's data centre and identify your assets and systems at any time.

Public Cloud: What is meant by a 'multi-ten-anted' system?

Both Private and Public Clouds are built on the concept of 'virtu-al machines', where one hardware server houses multiple smaller logically separate 'virtual' servers, or database instances. The term 'multi-tenanted' infrastructure is often used to describe the Cloud.

An analogy is similar to a block of apartments. Each tenant has access to specified parts of the building.

- In Public Cloud, you are renting an apartment, whereas

- In Private Cloud, you own (or have access to), broadly speaking, the whole building.

Focus on Public Cloud

This book focuses primarily on Public Cloud offerings, as this is where there the greatest potential exists for opacity over pricing, system capability, technical infrastructure limitations, governance and risk.

Examples of this include:

- You may not be able to access or review the setup of the physical infrastructure on which your systems operate. You may also have no specific assurances as to the location of the data, it could be in another country or not the country that you think it may be in!

- You also are unlikely to be able to inspect and review the provider's internal processes to satisfy yourself (or your auditors) of the robustness of their internal management processes.

Public Cloud is based on contractual obligations, and, at the end of the day trust that the Public Cloud vendor will meet these obligations. Chapter 5 covers this in more detail.

What about the risks in Public Cloud?

There are some obvious questions that need to be answered in relation to a Public Cloud solution. Typically these relate to the physical location of your system and data, retrieval of your data and system if needed, access controls over your data and systems, and the possible impact to your business should the Cloud provider go out of business.

There are some less obvious, but no less important risks that may be relevant to your organisation, some of which relate to your IT disaster recovery capabilities, system escrow, IT change control and software version management, to name but a few.

Chapter 8 covers this in more detail.

Which executive is accountable for Cloud systems in your organisation?

Whilst all stakeholders are entitled to hold and voice opinions on the selection and relevance of Cloud technologies for your organisation, it is important to have clear managerial account-abilities assigned when considering Cloud computing.

Cloud computing presents, by its very nature, compelling po-tential alternative solutions to problematic internally hosted IT systems. This, combined with the potential ability to bypass your IT department altogether (or at least minimise their in-volvement) offers to alleviate many of the frustrations experi-enced by business with the capacity and capability limitations of your own IT department.

Your organisation must be clear as to whom, ultimately is ac-countable for decisions relating to the deployment of Cloud computing, and your Executives should likewise be fully in-formed on the relevant issues of governance, risk and cost as-sociated with a shift to Cloud computing.

* * *

The takeaway messages from this chapter are:

- Cloud is a potentially disruptive technology, which brings simultaneously advantages, value and opportunity as well as risks. Be as fully informed as possible on both

- Understand *how* Cloud differs from prior IT trends

- Understand *why* Cloud has such potential appeal to line of business managers and users alike

- Understand the procurement and cost model for Cloud, and what implications it has for your organisation

- You may need a *greater* vigilance if adopting Public Cloud SaaS technologies for enterprise applications, when compared to on-premises applications

- Understand the conceptual difference between *Public* and *Private* Cloud computing models

- Public Cloud potentially introduces additional cost, technical, security and governance risks that are not normally associated with 'on-premises' IT systems and infrastructure

- Ensure there is a clear ownership and accountability at the top management level in your organisation for the adoption of Cloud technologies.

* * *

Chapter Two

The democratisation or consumerisation of IT

Some IT industry commentators and analysts have been drawing analogies between Cloud computing and technologies such as electric power for a number of years. Nicholas Carr in his book, "Does IT Matter?" (Harvard), predicted the consumerisation of IT and the emergence of utility style computing services as early as 2004.

In the example of the Electricity industry, as costs reduced through electricity generation and transmission technology advances, combined with a common standard for interoperability, opportunities opened up for forward-looking organisations to gain strong competitive advantages by using these new utility style services.

Once these services become universally accessible _with no material barrier to switching suppliers_, they become a true commodity.

The conventional 'on-premises' IT system

Since the large mainframe computer era of the '70s and before the advent of the Internet and subsequently Cloud computing, organisations generally had no alternative other than

17

to struggle with the cost and complexities of *on-premises IT systems*.

- The most obvious are the complex enterprise software projects that used 'off the shelf' IT systems (e.g. ERP Systems). Not only do the up front license costs require capital investment, organisations invariably have to upgrade data centre hardware and IT infrastructure on which the new or upgraded systems run.

Each installation of these enterprise systems is invariably lengthy, time consuming and expensive processes. At the end of the project, organisations hope that the investment results in a system that meets their business needs.

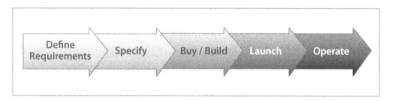

Figure 3: 'Traditional' On-premises system
commissioning process

In some 'on-premises' projects, during the lengthy time taken to design, configure and implement these systems, the business needs have changed, forcing further project delays as the software needs to be modified to meet these new requirements. This, in turn, adds to the cost and complexity of enterprise IT projects of this nature.

Cloud: Implement now, modify later

One of the value propositions of Cloud is the ability to implement a fully functioning system at *the start*, with minimal IT effort, and then potentially configure it later if needed.

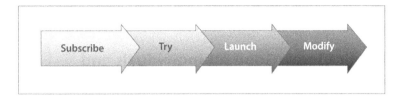

Figure 4: Simplified SaaS Cloud system commissioning process

Cloud computing: Making changes by configuration, not programming

An important concept to grasp at the core of Cloud computing is the mechanism by which system changes are implemented to meet your business' requirements.

Generally speaking, changes to the operation of software systems are made by either *programming* or *configuration*, or a combination of both.

*   *Programming* changes require specialised technical expertise in the underlying data structures, software program's languages and logic, whereas

*   *Configuration* can be done without any specific technical expertise.

Configuration changes affect how the system operates and appears to users, and is usually implemented by system administrators that access configuration maintenance screens. No change to the underlying software program is made.

This important concept has implications for how a Cloud system is managed and modified within your organisation, in that configuration generally provides limits to how far one can change the system's behaviour. To implement complex and detailed changes usually requires changes to the underlying programs, by making programming changes to the software itself.

Public Cloud: Good for individuals and organisations alike?

The Cloud computing model scales continuously from the individual to large enterprises, as the basis of service delivery and payment is, typically, on a per user per month basis. Simply put, the more you use, the more you pay.

This model has distinct appeal to both individuals and organisations alike.

Public Cloud technologies – targeting individuals (i.e. the public)

A single individual can access software systems that previously were only available to larger corporations.

These technologies are openly accessible by the general public. Examples of these are Gmail™ (Google's Cloud based mail and messaging system) and Facebook™ (the popular social networking site). These are common systems that are accessed, equally by all users. Whilst you can make some limited configuration changes to your instance of the system to meet your needs, the 'back-end' cannot be accessed or modified. You may, however, be able to utilise an eco-system of third party 'plug-ins' that extend functionality of the base system.

Likewise, in the business world, a large number of Cloud applications are available to organisations, including enterprise strength CRM (Customer Relationship Management) systems, content management systems, website portals, accounting and sales and marketing systems. These often have greatest appeal to start-up / small organisations and sole traders alike, and are typically, ideal candidates for the Public Cloud.

Public Cloud technologies – targeting enterprises

Organisations are able to implement enterprise-ready systems in very short timeframes, with minimal effort.

A fully functioning enterprise Cloud system can be configured and launched in days, with negligible start-up cost. This equates to the speed with which an individual would setup and configure their home PC!

In the eyes of many users and organisations, Cloud indeed offers a very compelling proposition. Potentially, you do not even need the involvement of your IT department to launch a business system.

Cloud and the changing role of IT

These influences, when combined, make for a somewhat difficult position for the conventional IT Department, who mostly have to still maintain a large pool of on-premise enterprise IT systems, keep the business going, and meet all the existing performance and compliance requirements of the organisation.

A by-product of the uptake of Cloud computing by organisations is the shift in the role of the conventional internally managed IT department.

When users and non-IT executives within organisations feel frustrated at the apparent slow speed of delivery of IT projects, systems that appear to be unnecessarily complex, not to mention the perceived high cost of IT support, the availability of alternative Cloud based serviced and systems have obvious appeal.

This is especially relevant, when the same users and non-IT executives have had their own, largely positive experiences in using Cloud computing as an individual *outside* of their organisation.

The value of Cloud is exemplified by:

- The ease of use and pervasiveness of technologies such as YouTube™, Gmail™, Facebook™, Linkedin™, Amazon™ and commercially robust and mature Cloud systems such as Salesforce™ and Google™, and

- The recent advent of the all-pervasive and powerful Cloud-enabled iPhones™, iPads™, Android™ and other mobile computing technologies which deliver individual consumers low cost, high value applications that can be deployed in minutes.

Is Cloud driving the transformation of the enterprise IT department?

The *reality* that IT systems can be low cost, easy to use, intuitive, and easy to implement in the personal lives of users translates directly to the *perception* and *expectation* that corporate or enterprise IT systems should be similarly easy to use, highly flexible, quick to implement and very low cost.

This perception is fuelled by two primary influences:

1. Individuals can access and experience the Cloud systems first hand, without needing IT involvement, and

2. Individuals are neither subject to the complexities of coordinating enterprise wide IT systems nor subject to the often stringent governance requirements and related mandates.

For organisations, these governance requirements do not change in moving enterprise systems to Cloud Computing.

Expecting IT departments to *not meet minimum due diligence and governance standards because the system is 'Cloud'*, requires a clear and unequivocal mandate from the Directors of the organisation to this effect.

Clearly, this does also not excuse enterprise IT departments that are poorly run from making poor decisions. Where IT departments are poorly run and badly aligned with the organisation's business plans and objectives, these issues need to be remedied.

Cloud computing may be a solution for part of your organisation's IT systems, but replacing your IT department with the Cloud is a strategy that needs extensive due diligence. Fix your organisation's IT management issues first, and then consider the Cloud, not the opposite.

What are the implications for procurement?

Due to the speed and relative ease of access to Cloud technologies, there is a risk of the unmanaged proliferation of Cloud technologies within organisations.

Where uncontrolled or unauthorised enterprise systems exist, so do the potential risks of information security problems, data integrity issues and compromises to the integrity of business processes.

There are a number of considerations in the selection and implementation of Cloud computing in your organisation, as discussed below.

Cloud is a technology and delivery mechanism choice. Manage it as such

Cloud technology contains your organisation's business logic and data, and as such it required some effort to maintain its:

23

- Accuracy

- Integrity

- Security

- Availability, and

- Interface to any other of your IT systems.

This is only part of the story, as there are some fundamental differences in approach to the risk, governance and commercial factors between 'on-premises' and Cloud computing systems. Chapters 6 and 8 cover this in more detail.

Have clear accountabilities over your Cloud implementation

Cloud systems are, in principle, no different from your existing on-premises IT systems. Someone (i.e. a specific Executive) in your organisation should have ultimate accountability for the cost, risk, use and overall governance of your enterprise systems.

Should a line-of-business departmental manager wish to select, implement and manage their own local enterprise systems, they should be able to do so only under the full visibility and rigours of your enterprise IT governance framework.

The importance of a clearly articulated Cloud procurement policy

Given that a SaaS Cloud system can be deployed in minutes and paid for out of the discretionary budget of a department within most organisations, it has the potential to expose the organisation to the risk of a 'viral Cloud'.

- A **viral Cloud** is characterised by a localised initial installation of a Cloud system (approved or otherwise!) in one part of the organisation, for a defined purpose. After a short period of time, access is progressively granted to others outside of the initial user pool as either the popularity of the system gains a foothold or others need to be given access to approve workflows, access documents, process information etc.

The low entry cost threshold for Cloud systems could mask the potential for significant future Total Cost of Ownership (TCO), unmitigated risk and breach of minimum governance standards.

Due to the ease of provisioning, access, configuration and use, there is increased risk of local divisions or business units in an organisation independently implementing Cloud technologies by using local, discretionary budgets, in the absence of an effective Cloud policy framework.

Organisations need to have effective Cloud computing policies to mitigate against the risks of ungoverned enterprise applications.

In the absence of a clearly articulated Cloud computing policy, traditional capital investment purchase processes can by bypassed, as individual user subscription costs are mostly treated as routine expenditure within the local business unit.

This has implications in multinational and multi-divisional organisations, where a local business unit wishes to implement an IT system to meet a local requirement.

Cloud: Low barrier to entry leading to vendor lock-in

Enterprise Cloud systems have a very low entry threshold. For a few dollars a month, a small but potentially influential pool of users could deploy an important application, which, when scaled out across the enterprise, could be prohibitively expensive.

Cloud computing has the potential to unleash the pent-up demand for better systems, improved reliability, less complexity, greater mobility and choice. All of these requirements are frequently valid at a local level, however organisations still require appropriate governance and due diligence processes to ensure that local decisions do not adversely impact the organisation as a whole.

IT departments often are in a unique position as they have a perspective of the *entire* organisation, and are required to balance the demands of a particular division or business unit against the requirements of the organisation as a whole.

* * *

The takeaway messages from this chapter are:

- The immediacy and universal access to Cloud technologies allows individuals and organisations alike, to implement systems 'on-demand'. This has potential implications for the procurement and project management approaches in the selection and implementation of enterprise IT systems

- Individual positive personal experiences in using Cloud systems are driving the demand for a similar level of service delivery by organisation's own IT departments

- Understand how and why Cloud has the potential to transform your view of the relevance and operation of your in-house IT department

- A cautious and unduly 'defensive' posture taken by your IT department to a move to Cloud computing needs assessment, and may be made on justifiable grounds. Investigate, don't dismiss or mandate.

* * *

* * *

Chapter Three

* * *

Cloud: Inversion of the IT business case? - *'buy before you try'*

This chapter explores the influences on the selection of Cloud computing systems, and how these can impact the effort and complexity of an implementation.

On-premises enterprise systems: The *buy-and-depreciate* approach

The process of purchasing and commissioning an enterprise business system typically involves a number of steps, such as the preparation of a business case, seeking approval and funding, followed by the implementation phase. Hopefully at some point in the future your organisation ends up with a system or technology that delivers the intended value sought.

These on-premises enterprise solutions usually require an initial capital outlay for software licenses, as well as infrastructure and project related costs.

This process can be lengthy, complex and often quite painful for organisations.

For large, enterprise-wide projects, this approach is inherently risky, in that after the lengthy, complex and expensive process of implementing a new enterprise system, you hope it meets your business' expectation and needs.

This approach is very much in the *buy-and-depreciate* regime.

Owning = low flexibility?

This conventional 'buy-and-depreciate' model for IT systems requires access to up front capital or finance.

Additionally, owning the IT systems:

º   Requires a commitment to future costs over the life of the system (the asset), which is typically over a number of years, and

º   There is a risk a financial write-off (and a reduction in profit) should there be a need to walk away from the system before it is fully depreciated and/or the benefits have been fully realised.

These factors all contribute to decreased flexibility, agility and potentially high exit cost considerations for on-premises enterprise IT systems.

Cloud enterprise systems: The '*buy before you try*' business model

As the barrier to entry into Public Cloud computing is almost non-existent, and a 'production ready' system can be made available almost immediately, there is a certain appeal in starting small, which has the immediate attraction of low initial cost.

Essentially, buy small then try the system. This is especially so in *standalone* Cloud systems, which do not have the complexity, cost, risk and governance issues associated with the connection or interfacing with other systems.

Impact of adding integration to other systems

The intrinsic value in enterprise IT systems lies in the *integration* of your various systems that allows for the streamlining of your business processes, elimination of waste, and allowing multiple stakeholders (e.g. staff, managers, business and channel partners, dealers, suppliers, customers) to have a *single source of the truth*.

It is highly probable that within the lifespan of the Cloud system, there will be a need to integrate/ interface the standalone Cloud system to other systems, whether they are other Cloud systems or on-premises to either:

*   Exchange data

*   Ensure consistency in naming and numbering conventions, data categorisations and groupings

*   Facilitating single-sign on between systems (which also avoids the effort involved in maintaining multiple identity management systems)

*   Ensuring consistency in access controls over various categories of data (for example, Staff personnel records, customer contract details, sales and pricing data)

*   Provide a consistent user interface, which is important from an organisation's branding perspective, not to mention consistency of screen navigation, which improves usability.

Now, consider issues associated with the integration of a standalone Cloud system with other systems, be they other Clouds or your on-premises systems.

The table below summarises a simplified case of the steps[1] that may be involved in the implementation of a Cloud system, both with and without interfaces to other systems.

Steps	AMOUNT OF IT INVOLVEMENT	
	Implementing a standalone Cloud software system	Implementing a Cloud software system with interfaces to other systems
Outline requirements	Minimal	Minimal
Find Cloud solutions	Minimal	Minimal
Define interface points	N/A	Moderate
Try Cloud pilot projects	Minimal	Low
Select Cloud system	Minimal	Low
Configure Cloud system	Minimal	N/A
Specify and build/buy interface application(s)	N/A	High
Test and implement interface programs	N/A	High
Define and implement change control processes	N/A	High
Configure Cloud system and interface application(s)	N/A	Moderate
Deploy	Minimal	Moderate

<u>Table 1:</u> Influence of integration in the implementation of Cloud computing

The additional complexities of implementing Cloud in this simple scenario are self-evident.

---

1   These steps, of course, are dependent on the specific nature of your organisation, type of project and are detailed purely for illustrative purposes

Managing runaway complexity

Another factor in driving up complexity, cost and risk, is the number of systems requiring to be interfaced to other systems.

The larger the number of system-system interfaces that are required, the maintenance effort and complexity increases exponentially.

Depending on the nature of the Cloud project, and the number and types of systems being interfaced to the Cloud system, the integration effort could be much larger than the effort in implementing the Cloud system itself!

This complexity arises in the coordination of the data mapping / conversion processes as well as the interface programs themselves. For example, each change in the on-premises system has the potential to require changes in both the interface system (whether by programming or configuration) and/or the Cloud system.

Whilst this exponential increase in the number of system-system interfaces is independent of whether the system is Cloud or not, the key determinant in Cloud systems is:

> The timing and types of changes and upgrades in Cloud computing are largely beyond your control.

Upgrades to Cloud systems occur on an ongoing basis, and are not always implemented at a date and time of your choosing.

This impact is primarily on the coordination of any upgrades in the interface programs.

Accepted standards in IT and business change control governance and compliance frameworks state that all changes should be tested to ensure at least nothing breaks, but that also there are no breaches in the security and integrity of the overall system.

How will Cloud help innovation?

Cloud systems can be very useful in supporting innovation initiatives in that:

- No up front capital is required

- Walk-away costs are minimised

- The opportunity for immediate and rapid scale-up to production exists without the need to provide working capital

- The team involved in the innovation project need not be burdened or distracted with the complexity, cost and effort of installing, configuring or maintaining IT infrastructure, and

- Generally, no programming is involved. Cloud systems offer users / administrators the ability to configure the system to meet their requirements, although there are limits to the amount of changes that can be implemented by configuration alone. The topic of making system changes through programming vs. configuration was discussed in Chapter 2.

If a pilot system is successfully deployed and implemented in the Cloud, and there is a high degree of enthusiasm to expand the initial deployment to full production, be aware of the costs, effort and risks associated with a full scale-up to production across your organisation. Chapters 7 and 8 cover this in more detail.

Depending on your usage profile, degree of integration with other systems, cost and risk profile, the Cloud system that was used for the successful prototype may NOT be the most appropriate choice for your full scale-up enterprise system.

For innovation projects involving Cloud computing, you are advised to set the stakeholder's expectations at the start of the project that a rapid scale-up to full blown production will involve a further review of the costs, risks and governance issues before a final decision will be made on the organisation-wide expansion to production

* * *

The takeaway messages from this chapter are:

• Due to the negligible entry and walk-away cost of Cloud computing, combined with its immediate access, Cloud offers organisations the ability to *buy before you try*

• As a general rule, there are no long-term, multi-year financial commitments in the Cloud offering, which is a fundamental shift from the conventional *buy-and-depreciate* model

• Closing down and migrating your on-premises IT systems and infrastructure to the Cloud may impact your profit due to write-offs

• Cloud can be of much value in supporting innovation initiatives, however a cost effective scaling-up to production from the pilot or prototype Cloud should not be assumed at the start

• Standalone Cloud systems offer the greatest flexibility. Integration to any other systems can add to the cost and complexity of a Cloud implementation.

* * *

* * *

Chapter Four

* * *

A field guide to the management of Cloud vendors

The sale of Cloud systems differs from the approach taken in the sale of on-premises IT systems in a number of ways.

Understanding these sales approaches is important in you being able to identify the strengths and weaknesses of the particular offer earlier in the sales cycle, thereby saving you time, effort, cost and potential surprises and frustration at a later date.

- The Cloud provider may not be delivering the implementation and support services. These services may be provided by a range of consultants and business partners, who may have varying degrees of technical expertise and experience

- Be aware of the risks, costs and benefits associated with the Cloud provider's eco-system of third party developers who market their applications independently of the provider, but on their Cloud platform. Examples of such markets include the Salesforce™ App Exchange and Google Android™ market.

Your approach to managing a prospective Cloud vendor's offerings is fundamental to exposing and understanding all the relevant aspects of their offerings to open scrutiny.

The following factors are outlined so that you are able to better frame the context of the vendor relationship, with a view to having a successful implementation on your part, and for the vendor to have a good reference customer!

The emphasis is on the 'product demonstration'

The primary weapon in the Cloud sales arsenal is the product demonstration. The provider is almost certainly able to demonstrate in real-time, the graphically rich, easy to read and understand user interface, which can be readily customised to the prospective customer's requirements.

The main hook is the 'wow' factor in showcasing how easy, intuitive and apparently low cost the system is.

Pet-shop marketing: Take the puppy home for the weekend

"Take the puppy home for the weekend, and if your kids are not happy with it, please bring it back!"

As the cost barrier to entry into the Cloud is typically very low for a pilot or start-up project, vendors are in a strong position to offer a low cost (or free) fully featured access to their offering at a moment's notice for a small number of target users.

This has these users immediately immersed in the (generally) easy to use, graphically rich and intuitive user interfaces.

- By comparison, neither your internal IT departments nor an on-premises system vendor are able do this in the same timeframe, where the installation, configuration and training processes can take some time.

The immediate consequence is that (assuming the software is functionally appropriate), users become rapid converts to the Cloud offering.

What will the puppy turn into?

Being swayed by very compelling and positive initial user experiences alone is not the basis for sound decision making for your organisation's enterprise applications. You hope that the puppy you took home does not grow up to be a Rottweiler.

In summary:

- Securing the sale is the primary short-term objective of the Cloud vendor

- Your objective, however, is to end up with a system that will deliver tangible and sustainable value to your organisation *over a period of time, with known cost and risk*.

'Top-down' sales strategy: Driving the wedge between IT and the business

When a vendor adopts a 'top-down' sales strategy, the primary targets are the senior non-IT executives, and line-of-business influential stakeholders.

If there is a groundswell of enthusiasm for the Cloud offering by executives and users, and especially where the IT department has been largely absent (for whatever reason) from the initial sales engagement, the risk is that any pre-existing fractures between IT and your business will expand to become larger.

Should this occur, there are a number of undesirable consequences, including:

• This has the potential of driving IT to become defensive, and

• Users becoming increasingly vocal and critical of the comparative non-delivery of systems and services from their own IT departments, based on their anticipated experience in using the Cloud system as offered by the vendor.

Ensure that you manage your IT executive(s) so that they, and their departments, play an active role in the Cloud discussions at each step in the process, from the start.

• If your IT team is reluctant to participate, identify the reasons for this as early as possible and deal with it

• If you are unsure that your IT department is willing to take the journey to Cloud willingly, listen carefully to the objections. The perceptions of 'job protection' aside, there may be some real technical limitations and fundamental governance concerns that the IT team are aware of, that has not been visible to the line of business stakeholders

• If your IT department hold ultimate accountability for enterprise IT system integrity, governance and risk, their concerns should be aired and scrutinised in the light of evidence based decision making. They should therefore have a casting vote on any key decisions relating to Cloud.

The role of your IT department in dealing with vendors

Your IT department's active involvement in each step of the entire Cloud vendor and solution selection process should be mandated.

- This mandate should be communicated with all managers in your organisation, so that the expectation has been set from the start

- Direct approaches by Cloud vendors to executives without the awareness or support of the IT department should be prevented.

The key questions that have to be answered are:

- Which executive in your organisation is accountable for the selection, procurement and governance of enterprise IT systems, irrespective of whether they be Cloud or not?

- If your organisation operates under a federated IT structure, (that is differing divisions or business units are accountable for all or part of their IT infrastructure or systems) who has accountability over the risk and governance of Cloud technologies in these divisions or business units?

- What is your approach to the management of unsolicited offers by Cloud vendors?

No part of your organisation should be actively engaging with Cloud vendors without the transparent collaboration and engagement of your IT division.

The heart of the overall governance of your enterprise IT systems rests on the appropriate balance between the selection, implementation, integration and ongoing management of systems and technologies that meet your defined business needs. IT departments are usually the primary functions that are capable of providing this capability to the required level of detail.

* * *

The takeaway messages from this chapter are:

- Involve your IT department in *all* Cloud discussions from day one

- Do not be easily swayed on the basis of a compelling software demonstration alone.

- Consider the evidence behind the demonstration with the full involvement of your IT division

- If your IT executives are reluctant to participate in the Cloud discussion, identify the reasons for this and deal with them. Their active participation is critical to the success of your Cloud implementations

- Implement an organisation wide Cloud procurement policy and communicate this to all stakeholders across your organisation

- Organisations must clearly define who holds accountability for the risks and costs associated with Cloud implementation.

✳ ✳ ✳

Chapter Five

✳ ✳ ✳

Cloud vendor contract and legal considerations

The contract you sign with your Cloud service provider is very important, as, unlike on-premises IT systems, you typically only have rights to retrieve the data and information that you have loaded into the system. Moreover, your Cloud system is external to your organisation, and is an entity over which you have no physical control.

The following factors should be considered in your vendor selection and negotiations:

Understand your Cloud vendor's contract

Given the maturing nature of the Cloud market:

- Cloud provisioning contracts may not be at the expected level of maturity to meet the general legal, regulatory and commercial contracting requirements as applicable to your organisation, and

- There has been little legal precedence in respect of Cloud contract legal rulings.

At the end of the day, all you have is a contract – it should be substantive and enforceable.

Figure 5: Is the contract you have with your Cloud vendor substantive and in your best interests?

Should the vendor relationship irrevocably fail for whatever reason and your best interests are not protected and enforceable under the terms of the contract, a serious risk to your business may exist. Transferring *your applications* from the incumbent Cloud supplier to another may not be possible and is most likely to not be a trivial exercise if it were possible.

Contract duration

It is in the best interests of the vendor to secure your business for as long as possible. This may not be in *your* best interests.

This contradicts the principle of SaaS where you consume these services as it suits *you, for a period of time that suits you.*

There are a few factors that should be taken into consideration, some of which are:

- If this is truly SaaS, why would you need to commit to a contract for a long period of time, if that does not suit you? You, as a consumer, should be able to opt-out whenever it suits you!

- You should also be able to scale up and _down_ as you see fit – after all it is SaaS!

- SaaS is often marketed on the basis of a 'per user per month' fee, so insist on being billed on a monthly basis only during the contract period, and

- Pay specific attention to any automatic renewal clauses. You may prefer to be in control of any contract renewals.

Request a copy of the draft contract as early as possible in the sales process

Vendors may attempt to maximise the opportunity of a successful sale by deferring discussion of the full details of the supply and services contract to the latter stages of the sale cycle.

This minimises the probability of compliance, risk, ownership and other objections being raised, which could jeopardise the sale. The further down the sales pre-selection process one progresses, the less likely the apparently minor contractual niceties will be seen as problematic, should there be a groundswell of enthusiasm in favour of a particular vendor's system.

- The sales and procurement cycles can be time consuming and resource intensive. All that effort could be wasted if there is a major impediment in your organisation signing the vendor's contract at a late stage in the proceedings.

What form does the contract take?

Cloud vendors may offer you a master contract, which refers to web pages that may have terms and conditions that change without your knowledge.

- Insist on an all encompassing, fully encapsulated contract that cannot change for the intended contract period

- No reference should be made to the vendor's website for contract details. If necessary, print out, date and initial each page of the agreement terms as they appear at the time that the main agreement is signed, and amend the terms of the main agreement if needed to refer to that specific documentation.

The 'I accept' logon checkbox

Be aware of the presentation of and rote acceptance of any terms and conditions during the login process in accessing the system.

- This may take to the form of a popup banner advising the individual of the relevant terms and conditions, or

- The user may need to take a specific action by actioning an 'I accept the terms and conditions for the use of this system' checkbox (or similar).

These online conditions may supersede some of your existing contract terms and conditions. Ensure that your master written contract's terms and conditions always extinguish any such login terms and conditions in all instances, in perpetuity.

Contract variations

Cloud vendors prefer a standardised contract. Vendors resist any contract amendments, as any amendments may require them to provide non-standard services, which contradicts the utility computing model. Most Cloud providers refuse to do so, unless the potential customer has considerable buying power or influence.

If the contract cannot be changed, then the expectations of your organisation's stakeholders need to be managed accordingly.

Considerations for multinational corporations

If you are a subsidiary within a multinational organisation, there are a number of factors that may influence how you subscribe to Cloud services including:

- Existence of a global policy mandating the use of a SaaS System that exists in a foreign legal jurisdiction (to ensure consistency of global systems and standards).

    ○ Should some of *your* customers include government or commercial organisations that preclude you from allowing any of *their* information being resident on *your* systems leaving the country, how would you remedy this situation?

- Your parent company has negotiated a global subscription pricing structure that does not include some specific services that you wish to utilise.

    ○ How can you negotiate acceptable terms for these services if the vendor understands that you are committed to using them, and price-gouging is a possibility?

Chapter 10 covers this in more detail.

Other contract considerations

The costs of seeking remedies under a contract in foreign jurisdictions may be time consuming and prohibitively costly. Be aware of the potential costs and complexity associated with seeking remedies for persistent and material breaches of your Cloud vendor's agreement. These may present an obstacle in you seeking remedies in the first instance.

Additionally, pay special attention to aspects such as:

Jurisdictional issues

- Are there any trans-border data transmission issues?

Security and technical considerations

- Are you aware or concerned about the data transmission encryption standards and methods used, and if so, what information does the contract contain in this regard?

Vendor structure and ownership issues

- The ownership structure of the Cloud provider may be a private, joint venture, or may have an opaque ownership structure. Does this concern you?

- What are the implications should the Cloud provider be acquired by a direct competitor of *your* organisation?

- If the Cloud service provider is sold, acquired by another organisation, what contract transition issues exist between the outgoing and incoming providers, either immediately, or at contract renewal?

Service levels, performance penalties and credits

- Are service levels and the financial penalties for non-performance explicitly stated, measurable, and material to the degree and type of non-performance?

- If offered, are subscription credits suitable compensation to your organisation in the event of a material non-performance by the Cloud provider?

- What service level and service availability standards are written into the contract? How is non-availability measured in terms of service credits for such non-availability – per incident or cumulative? For example, if your Cloud provider measures and offers compensation on a non-availability per event basis up to a defined time period (e.g. 10 minutes per event), how would you seek compensation should multiple and persistent events occur below this threshold?

Legislative, regulatory and compliance issues[2]

- What National Privacy Principles (NPPs) apply under the Privacy Act (*The Privacy Act 1988 (Australian Commonwealth)* to your instance of the Cloud system?

- What document and information retention requirements cannot be met by the Cloud provider under the applicable Federal or State laws? *(Corporations Act 2001 (Australian Commonwealth)*

- Are there any Industry specific regulations that apply to your organisation? For example, *APRA (Australian Prudential Regulation Authority)*

- What rights do you, as a customer, have to request an independent external audit of the vendor's infrastructure, or seek evidence of existing reputable and independently verifiable regulatory or standards compliance? (The 'right to audit' clause)

---

2   Or laws that exist under differing international jurisdictions

- Which foreign legal jurisdictions apply? This may depend on the location of primary and backup Cloud services, company ownership and structure.

Contractual rights and obligations

- Can you explicitly confirm who has title over *your* intellectual property that is vested in data schemas, business logic or programs that *you have written that exist on the vendor's infrastructure*, i.e. can these programs be re-deployed to other clients, without your approval, to the benefit of the vendor or any other party?

- What warranties and warranty exclusions or limitations apply to services offered, and are there any conflicts with prevailing commercial laws[3]? Some laws offer rights that cannot be excluded or exchanged

- What are the loss or limitation provisions under the contract? Are consequential losses relevant to your organisation? For example, should your Cloud provider suffer a major system malfunction that prevents you from accessing your system for an extended period of time, your organisation may suffer brand and reputation damage, let alone not be able to survive should you not have alternative backup arrangements in place

- What guarantees exist that all data is destroyed at contract end – including all cyclical backups, data mirrors? Are you able to seek independent verification of the destruction or removal of your information, should it be deemed very sensitive?

---

3 For example, Competition and Consumer Act 2010 *(Australian Commonwealth)*, Schedules 2, Sections 60 and 61, or applicable laws in other international legal jurisdictions

- What are the transition out terms and conditions? Data may need to be accessed for a defined period (e.g. 10 years) after an event giving rise to litigation. Once you have transitioned out of the Cloud system, you may have your low level data, but no easy way of interpreting the data as the applications and business logic has been left behind in the Cloud

- What part do the multiple parties in the Cloud infrastructure stack play in the provider's contract, and what are the implications should the provider switch a major sub-system of their Cloud system without informing you, and this change adversely impacts your organisation? Is this important for you to know?

Types of users and related cost factors

- Ensure your contract is explicit about the costs associated with all possible user *types*. Specify the types of user categories and user groups that you are likely to encounter during the life of the system (e.g. public occasional user, internal staff user, anonymous user, authenticated self-registering users, administrators, programmers, etc.)

- Identify what costs (if any) are associated with the deployment of the Cloud system through handheld mobile devices (Android™, iPhone™, iPad™ etc), whether they be provided by the vendor, or written by you on the vendor's system

- Negotiate an upper limit of the year-on-year percentage increases in costs, capped to the prevailing national inflation rate, CPI or other independent benchmark.

* * *

The takeaway messages from this chapter are:

- Ensure your contract is an all encompassing document that perpetually extinguishes any terms and conditions that may exist on the vendor's website, or are presented to users when accessing the system

- The only recourse you have in the Cloud is your contract. Pay specific attention to the terms of the contract, and what their implications are for your business under likely or possible business scenario's

- Understand the terms of the vendor's contract in detail as early on as possible in the buy cycle

- Know what remedies you are able or likely to be able to enforce in the event of a breach of the vendor's agreement

- Be aware of any international or multi-jurisdictional factors in your contract.

* * *

* * *

Chapter Six

* * *

Opinions... Opinions.... Who do I trust?

Currently, there are a wealth of opinions, misunderstandings, and some degree of opacity as to what Cloud is, how it can be deployed and where its intrinsic value lies for organisations.

Cloud computing, and SaaS in particular, has its value and a place in organisations, however, its potential limitations and risks should not be lightly dismissed.

It is critical to the *successful* outcome of *your* enterprise Cloud projects, that both the upside potential and challenges are assessed in an objective manner.

'Cloud-huggers' and 'tin-huggers'

There are a number of Cloud technology evangelists, who promote Cloud with a clear bias.

Also known as 'Cloud-huggers', they are sometimes dismissive of, or understate some of the concerns inherent in SaaS Cloud infrastructures. Conversely, individuals that show a clear reluctance to embrace Cloud technologies are immediately seen as 'anti-Cloud', and resistant to change. Sometimes termed 'tin-huggers', they have a clear preference for on-premises IT equipment (or at least IT equipment, whose whereabouts can be identified with certainty).

Unfortunately, such generalisations and polarisation is a potential distraction for organisations trying to assess the relevance of Cloud for *their* organisation's *specific* situation.

Cloud is a technology and delivery mechanism choice, not a philosophy!

Whether opinions are offered or sought from your own IT department, industry analysts, Cloud vendors, 'Cloud-huggers', 'tin-huggers', Cloud service providers, consultants, IT system integrators or managed service providers. It is important to see Cloud as a *technology and delivery choice*, not a *point of philosophical difference*.

*   Some traditional IT hosting service providers have done a 'Cloud-wash' of their offering without fundamentally changing their internal capabilities or offerings. This is analogous to a 'rebranding' initiative. Be aware of what Cloud is, and when Cloud is not Cloud.

The ultimate proof: Proof of concept trail

The usually compelling position by 'Cloud-huggers' that Cloud is quick, easy and low cost to implement and maintain in the organisation, should be tested by providing seed funding to implement a tightly controlled technical pilot / proof of concept (POC) in your organisation.

*   As organisation's situations differ, the assumption that 'because it works somewhere else, it'll work here' may not necessarily be valid

- Only by conducting a limited scope, proof of concept trail which focuses on the governance and technical issues, will your organisation be able to provide irrefutable evidence that all critical technical components such as system integration, single sign-on integration, security and change control will work as they are purported to, and that *your organisation's minimum security and governance criteria are met*

- This POC trial need only, for example, transact 1 customer order, for 1 customer, with 1 product, that will be delivered to 1 address, which will trigger 1 invoice, that will be paid, and cash allocated.

The role of consultants: pre-sale, selection and implementation

Consultants are a valuable asset to an organisation that may not have the skills, resources and experience to appropriately assess Cloud.

As the Cloud marketplace matures, and whilst organisations as well as the IT industry gain further experience in implementing this new technology, there are an ever increasing number of consulting organisations that are acquiring the necessary skills to be in a position to provide professional consulting or advisory services.

Advisory vs. Consulting

If your consultant has no interested in deriving revenue from the implementation of your chosen technology, and you engage them in a purely advisory capacity, there is a high degree of probability that their recommendations are in your best interests, and are almost certain to be independent. This assumes, of course that they have a deep and broad understanding of Cloud technologies from a cost, risk and governance perspective, and not unduly focussing on the upside potential.

Scenario:

- Your *consultant* expects to derive $100,000 revenue from helping you implement vendor A's solution, and $10,000 revenue from vendor B's solution. What would their preference be? What's good for you or what's good for the consultant?

- Your *advisor* charges a $30,000 flat fee for the analysis of your needs, requirements assessment, risk and governance profiling, and suggests a process by which vendor's offerings can be assessed, verified and assured. You may also receive advice you on which consultants are appropriate for the engagement.

Question: Which is the best option for your organisation?

Key attributes to look for in Cloud consultants:

There are a number of attributes that you should consider in engaging consultants. Not all of these attributes are relevant to your specific project.

Expertise in the *assessment* of Cloud technologies in the *context* of your organisation

Consultants must have a demonstrated and proven expertise and experience in the technical complexities, commercial realities and governance issues of Cloud technologies.

Some consultants may have the *technical* expertise in the implementation and integration of Cloud systems however may lack skills in the financial, commercial, regulatory and governance aspects.

No two enterprise systems are the same, as each organisation differs in respect of:

- How the Cloud system is configured and used,

- The business model for the organisation, as well as their

- Business processes.

Because a particular Cloud system has worked well in another organisation, does not automatically mean that it will be appropriate for your organisation.

Integrated approach

It is critical that both you and/or your chosen consultants have the ability to integrate all the factors and influences, not just the technology focussed ones, in recommending a solution. These include:

- Governance

- Risk

- Lifecycle cost

- Commercial considerations

- Regulatory and statutory requirements

- Your business strategy, and possibly

- Experience in your particular industry.

If your consultant is helping you in the selection of an enterprise Cloud system, they should have the skills to be able to synthesise and integrate all these factors.

Technology agnostic

Assured independence of opinion is the core value that consultants can provide. If your consultant shows a bias towards a particular type of Cloud technology *before* commencing the engagement, you should, with justification, be concerned, that your organisation's best interests are not being served.

Vendor independence

A source of revenue for many consulting organisations is often derived from the implementation and support services associated with certain Cloud technologies. This often leads to them being 'certified' in the vendor's technology, and in doing so they may show a bias towards a particular vendor.

Agility vs. methodology bound

Whilst discovery, selection and engagement methodologies are important for the assurance of a successful result, consultants who rigorously are bound by their methodologies are sometimes not able to move quickly to arrive at an effective solution. This can lead to lengthier and higher cost engagements.

- A prescriptive methodology is sometimes used by consulting organisations as a way of:

  o Raising additional revenue through the licensing of a proprietary methodology or assessment framework, and

  o Institutionalising core skills and expertise so that lesser qualified and experienced consultants are able to 'follow the process' to ensure a defined outcome.

* * *

The takeaway messages from this chapter are:

- Seek evidence, not opinions before making important decisions

- If you are not sure what questions to ask the vendor(s), find someone who has experience and absolute independence and ask them

- Seek hard evidence to support the proposition that Cloud is easy to implement and to integrate with your existing systems by completing a technical proof of concept trial. This should, by definition, be low cost, fast and efficient. If it is not, then the rest of the project is unlikely to be low cost, fast or efficient

- Assess when best to engage advisors and/or consultants

- Be able to assess the skills, competencies and capabilities of your chosen consultant.

* * *

* * *

Chapter Seven

* * *

Low cost - 'Like a sub-prime mortgage?'

Cloud computing often has immediate appeal. In a recent article I wrote in CIO magazine, I drew a number of analogies between enterprise Cloud computing and a sub-prime mortgage in an attempt to trigger some debate in the CIO and business communities alike.

Analogies included: some product opacity, risk being downplayed up front, the promise of continual rising value / reducing cost, easy to get in, perhaps not so easy to get out and some pressure on not being left behind.

- You really want that house (software system), and you just love the kitchen (easy to use), however don't worry about checking the plumbing!

A key tenet of Cloud computing is low cost, and this chapter expands on this crucial aspect of Cloud computing to illustrate that this is not always the case. Moving from a capital purchase to a perpetual subscription model also presents a challenge to the unaware in that the low initial cost may prove to be anything but that, over a period of time.

This has serious ramifications in organisations of scale, where a *per user per month* costing model may be extremely costly when compared to a *concurrent* license costing model.

The heart of the issue is being able to satisfactorily answer this apparently trivial question when comparing two functionally similar systems:

- Is a Cloud system that costs $100 / user / month, cheaper than an on-premises system that cost $1 Million up front?

This talks to the heart of the cost of enterprise Cloud computing – that is:

Opex instead of Capex

Cost is not the whole picture

In this chapter, the primary focus is on cost, and the mechanisms, assumptions and implications for the varying pricing models. Of course, cost is only one of the determinants of the overall decision whether to implement Cloud or any other systems, however given the relative importance of cost, it warrants a more in-depth discussion.

Importance of the approach to licensing models

A driver in the Total Cost of Ownership (TCO) of an enterprise IT system is the software license or subscription cost. These software license or subscription models can take on various forms, and are discussed in more detail below.

What are the differences between concurrent user, named user or server-based software licensing models?

A determinant on the cost effectiveness of Cloud SaaS systems is the usage intensity per user. The way licensing and subscription models are used can have profound impacts on your software costs, and depends on the length of time that you operate the system. This is illustrated by the following examples:

Software licensing option #1: Named user subscription

How does it work?

The named user subscription model defines what usage you **could** have used. One subscription is assigned to a unique logon (user name), irrespective of how many times the users access the system.

The analogy:

This model licenses you for the number of light bulbs in your house, whether you switch them all on, or some, some of the time.

Example:

Your subscription charge is $50/month per user, and you have 500 named users. That's an annual cost of $300,000 per year, irrespective of how many times the users access the system.

This pricing model is the accepted standard for Cloud providers.

Software licensing option #2: Concurrent usage

How does it work?

The concurrent user subscription model defines what the maximum usage is permitted at *any point in time*. Subscriptions are not assigned to any unique logon (user name). Typically, there is no restriction to the number of logons (user name).

The analogy:

This model licenses you for the number of light bulbs you have switched on at any point in time in your house. You can have as many light fittings as you like, there is no restriction.

Example:

At any one point in time, there are no more than 10% of users using the system. You are therefore licensed for 50 concurrent users. Assuming the subscription charge is the same[4], but for concurrent usage, the annual cost falls to $30,000.

This pricing model is sometimes used for on-premises Enterprise systems.

Software licensing option #3: Server based license

How does it work?

You pay for the license to run the software system on a server[5]. There is no limit on the number of concurrent or named

---

4   This is unlikely, however the concurrent usage subscription cost has been left unchanged to illustrate the concept.
5   Usually, licenses are purchased per 'core'. Think of a 'core' as a cylinder in an engine. If you need to provide more power, you purchase and switch on more cylinders. Modern servers operate on multi-core processors, so switching on

users. The limiting factor is the performance capacity of the server. An overloaded server may cease to operate or the performance degrades causing excessively slow response times.

The analogy:

This model licenses you for the whole house. You can install as many light fittings into the house, and switch on as many of these lights on at any one time, however, your power to the house is limited. Past a certain point, all the lights start dimming and you need to purchase more power.

Example:

A server based license for an application costs you $500,000 up front. The server is able to comfortably support 500 users concurrently on the system, without any degradation in performance. You also depreciate this up-front license purchase cost over a 36 month period.

The comparative software costs:

The following table summarises the three year total cost of the three options:

The three year total cost is therefore as follows:	
Option #1: Named user subscription model	$900,000
Option #2: Concurrent usage model	$90,000
Option #3: Server based license model:	$500,000

more processors is a simple technical exercise and requires no upgrades or service interruption.

This simplistic example illustrates the potential impact that alternative licensing models have on the total cost of a solution.

Comparing costs between Cloud and on-premises: The two questions

To get a true perspective of which presents a better deal, the two questions that need answering are:

1. What is the life expectancy of the system?

2. Can you compare the Cloud and on-premises costs on a like-for-like cost basis?

Each question is discussed in more detail below.

Question 1: What is the life expectancy of the system?

A determinant on the Total Cost of Ownership (TCO) is the annualised cost over the life of the system.

At what point does the TCO break-even point for 'own and depreciate' vs. perpetual subscription costs occur, if at all?

Consider the following simplistic scenario:

- Cloud: Annual costs are $200,000 / year perpetual

- On-Premises: Capital cost $550,000 + 15%/year software maintenance from years 2 onwards

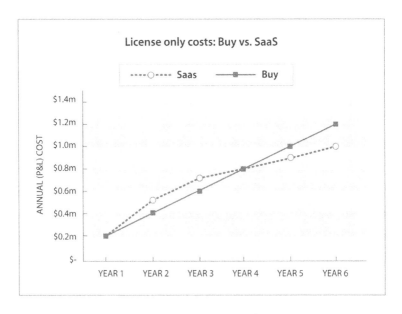

Figure 6: Buy and depreciate vs. subscription (SaaS) breakeven point

In this simple example, the breakeven appears at the 4th year after which Cloud becomes more expensive.

So:

- If you are planning to have the system for 2 years, Cloud is cheaper by $50,000 after 24 months

- If you are planning to have the system for 5 years, Cloud is more expensive by $20,000.

Question 2: Can you compare the Cloud and on-premises costs on a like-for-like cost basis?

In order to be able to draw valid cost comparisons between Cloud and on-premises systems, you need to understand *how* these costs are accounted for.

- Organisations looking to replace internal, integrated IT systems with a Cloud equivalent purely on the basis of cost saving, should determine the *cost per user per month per application (PUPMA)* for their own systems first

- Only then can a true comparison be made as to which is the more cost effective.

To explore this concept, consider the following simplified scenario:

* * *

Scenario:

Acme Inc. runs its own IT systems on-premises and the IT Department's total monthly costs are reported as:

General Ledger Account	Total / GL Account
Hardware maintenance	$12,000
Software maintenance	$11,100
Staff	$24,750
Utility	$11,850
Rent	$7,600
Consultants	$30,650
Depreciation	$23,500
Amortisation	$18,000
Staff training	$11,750
Data centre	$18,300
Total cost on-premises systems / month	**$169,500**

Figure 7: Chart of accounts for Acme Inc's IT department

Acme Inc also believes that there are significant savings to be realised by moving three of their enterprise systems to Cloud computing. These being:

- Email

- CRM, and

- Website.

The respective Cloud vendors are quoting

- $20/user /month for Acme's 'email in the Cloud'

- $100/user /month for Acme's 'CRM in the Cloud'

- $20/user/month for Acme's 'Web portal in the Cloud'

Question: Which is the better deal from a cost perspective for each of the three systems?

---

* * *

Discussion:

Based on an analysis of the how the costs components were apportioned to the various existing on-premises applications, the following costs *per application per month* were derived, for all applications.

To illustrate the approach taken, the analysis is broken down to a step-by-step process, as detailed below:

Step #1: Find out the total cost per application:

Transforming known IT costs to a total cost per application requires a combination of skills and knowledge in both:

- **Finance and accounting**
  Understanding the allocation of costs of utilities, depreciation, overheads, amortisation and all other IT costs within your organisation's accounting systems.

- **IT application and IT architecture**
  Knowledge of how, the various applications and systems are structured, and which servers and infrastructure they run on.

This exercise may not be a trivial task depending on the complexity of your organisation's IT systems and infrastructure, however once completed, your organisation will have full visibility and granularity of how much each system costs, in detail.

In this simple scenario, the costs for each of the following systems was calculated and shown in the table below. Note that the total cost of all applications reconciles with the total departmental cost of $169,500.

General Ledger Account	EMAIL	ERP	CRM	WAREHOUSE	WEBSITE	Total / GL Account
Hardware maintenance	$1,000	$250	$2,000	$6,250	$2,500	**$12,000**
Software maintenance	$750	$1,500	$1,250	$1,600	$6,000	**$11,100**
Staff	$2,500	$10,000	$2,500	$3,750	$6,000	**$24,750**
Utility	$1,250	$600	$2,750	$6,000	$1,250	**$11,850**
Rent	$750	$600	$2,750	$3,000	$500	**$7,600**
Consultants	$1,650	$7,500	$4,000	$6,000	$11,500	**$30,650**
Depreciation	$500	$10,500	$2,500	$4,000	$6,000	**$23,500**
Amortisation	$2,500	$1,250	$2,500	$7,500	$4,250	**$18,000**
Staff training	$1,000	$250	$2,750	$3,500	$4,250	**$11,750**
Data centre	$2,800	$2,000	$3,000	$4,500	$6,000	**$18,300**
Total Cost / System on-premises	**$14,700**	**$34,450**	**$26,000**	**$46,100**	**$48,250**	**$169,500**

Move these applications to the cloud?

Figure 8: Cost analysis per application per month
for Acme Inc's IT department

Step #2: Identify the number of users of each of the various applications:

This should be based on the total number of users, as most Cloud providers' subscription models are based on named users.

	EMAIL	CRM	WEBSITE
Number of Users	500	500	2,500

Figure 9: Acme Inc's total number of users
per application per month

Step #3: Calculate the cost *per user* for each of the on-premises applications, by dividing the total cost of each application by the number of users:

	EMAIL	CRM	WEBSITE
Total Cost on-premises systems / month	$14,700	$26,000	$48,250
Number of users	500	500	2,500
Cost / user / month - On Premises	**$29.40**	**$52.00**	**$19.30**

Figure 10: Acme Inc's per users per application cost per month

Step #4: Detail the per user per month costs for the three systems that are contenders for Cloud computing, based on the pricing provided by the vendors.

69

	EMAIL	CRM	WEBSITE
Cost / user / month - Cloud	$20.00	$100.00	$20.00

Figure 11: Cloud provider's quoted cost per month

Step #5: You are now in a position to compare the costs of the on-premises systems with the Cloud equivalent. This is detailed in the following table, which shows that the Cloud alternative is not always the lowest cost:

	EMAIL	CRM	WEBSITE
Cost / user / month - On Premises	$29.40	$52.00	$19.30
Cost / user / month - Cloud	$20.00	$100.00	$20.00
Cheapest alternative	Cloud	On Premises	Marginal

Figure 12: Comparing Cloud and on-premises
on a like-for-like basis.

* * *

In summary

Only once your existing IT costs are transformed to *a per user per month per application* basis (PUPMA), are you able to draw a direct cost comparison on a 'like-for-like' basis between your on-premises system and the Cloud equivalent.

The effort invested in completing this exercise will ensure that you make the correct cost decision.

Cost certainty over the lifespan of the Cloud system

The costs of all enterprise systems vary over their lifecycle. Supplemental software may be purchased, some systems de-commissioned new systems implemented, and so on.

In the Cloud computing model, the total costs of the system are often not limited to the core system's monthly subscription cost. Cloud vendors can also offer a rich range of applications, plug-ins and extension features that have been written by a range of individuals, vendor's business partners or independent software organisations.

These additional systems provide very useful extensions to the core functionality offered by the provider's system, and may also avoid you needing to implement complicated or costly workarounds.

To determine the Total Cost of Ownership (TCO) of the Cloud application, you should investigate the known costs associated with:

- Purchasing additional 'plug-in' software (as needed) that can be sourced from third parties and/or independent vendors that form part of the Cloud vendor's eco-system (Similar to the Apple iStore™)

- Integrating the Cloud application with other systems, whether they be other Cloud systems or on-premises

- The Cloud implementation project itself, to include all aspects such as staff travel, consultants, security review, legal and contract review, training (including system administrators, IT developers, end-users) as well as IT staff outplacement and redundancy and/or re-skilling as required.

- Potential foreign exchange losses (or gains) if the Cloud vendor requires billing in a foreign currency

- Re-designing and changing your internal business processes that are need to use the new system

- Updating user documentation (procedures, policies)

- Data migration and conversion to exchange data with the Cloud.

Third party Cloud providers

Other considerations relate to the Cloud vendor *eco-system*, where independent software developers and companies develop separate applications *on the Cloud vendor's environment*.

These applications are all written on the Cloud vendor's infrastructure, and conform to the technical standards mandated by that vendor. They are generally not transferable to other Cloud vendors.

In this instance, the sale is negotiated between you and the independent developer.

- This is analogous to the Apple iStore™, where iPad™ and iPhone™ users can download and install software applications written by a range of people and organisations, however they *only* operate on the Apple™ proprietary technology.

Check with the vendor if there are any other access charges that they may levy over and above those associated with their core system.

It is in the Cloud vendor's interests to develop a dynamic and rich eco-system of add-on systems, which paradoxically also tends to increases your lock-in to their particular brand of Cloud.

Unrestricted or enterprise Cloud offerings – Good value?

Some vendors offer an unrestricted or enterprise category of subscription for their larger customers. The terms of such an offering typically require a multi-year contract to be signed.

- This *contradicts* the premise of software 'as a service', where your organisation is billed for what it *actually* uses

- In essence, the unrestricted or enterprise style multi-year license is similar to the 'buy-and-depreciate' alternative, as there are contract early termination penalty costs, which are analogous to asset write-offs in the on-premises equivalent.

Unrestricted does not equate to unlimited, or 'all-you-can-eat' offerings. No Cloud system has unlimited capacity and processing power, so expect to have some performance and capacity limits placed on your Cloud system.

Know and understand the difference.

Switching to the Cloud: Cheap and easy?

Be aware of the factors that influence the cost, complexity or effort of transferring your existing systems to the Cloud. Some of these factors include:

- Identify the cost write offs of any software, hardware being decommissioned

- Be aware of all existing hardware, software and service maintenance exit costs

- Be aware of any critical IT staff dependencies *during* the migration, especially if they are to be made redundant on the completion of the project

- Clearly identify the costs and effort associated with data migration to the Cloud

- Meticulously review the migration project plan, including rollback planning.

Likely to change usage patterns in the future?

Be fully aware of the cost and performance implications of changing the number and types of users once implemented.

Organisations need to be acutely aware of any other performance, size and other limitations imposed by the vendor.

- If your systems require much higher processor loads (e.g. introducing mathematically intensive calculations), you may breach performance limits which may result in, either:

  a) A physical limit on the amount of processing power, resulting in unacceptable slow response times, or

  b) Additional costs to you, as the vendor will need to bring additional processor power online.

Summary

In summary, this chapter attempts to illustrate some of the factors that influence the cost of Cloud computing in organisations.

The apparent simplicity and low cost of the pricing model offered by many vendors masks the potential complexity and cost of a particular solution, once fully implemented.

The message here is to know what you are getting into, understand your costs, know how the costs are derived, and understand your options.

Having said that, once you understand your cost exposure as best you can, you are then in a very clear position to assess the return on investment in any significant investment in Cloud computing, and allow you to progress with increased certainty.

＊ ＊ ＊

The takeaway messages from this chapter are:

- Know the Total Cost of Ownership in detail of any Cloud System

- Compare the Cloud to other systems (whether on-premises or other Cloud systems) on the same basis: per user per month per application (PUPMA), if relevant

- Know the total project implementation costs in detail

- Know your Cloud exit costs and strategy

- Understand the number and categories of users, as well as your most likely usage patterns over the life of the system, and model these costs accurately

- Understand possible cost exposure by the purchase of additional third party applications and plug-in's

- Be aware of the implications of signing up for an *unrestricted* or *enterprise* style Cloud subscription

- Know and understand your cost exposures for differing usage patterns

* * *

* * *

Chapter Eight

* * *

Risk – the gorilla in the dark room?

Entrusting your organisation's systems to 'someone out there on the Internet' is somewhat a step of faith for many, however the benefits of moving to a Cloud environment could far outweigh the risks.

In order to objectively assess these risks, you need to expose and understand all the known risks as they relate to your organisation.

Additionally, as Cloud computing is evolving constantly, you may need to review your risks on a regular basis.

Risk: The obvious questions

The most commonly asked and discussed questions include:

Where is you data located?

Your data may reside overseas and be subject to one or more international jurisdictions. This occurs when systems are replicated, or mirrored across differing data centres in the Cloud provider's infrastructure.

Depending on your Cloud provider, they may be unwilling to identify, specifically, where your data is residing.

Can you get your data back easily?

It is an accepted norm with Cloud providers that your data is your property, and providers offer tools and methods of being able to extract all of your data from their Cloud system with relative ease.

Who can access your data?

Cloud providers own the infrastructure on which your systems, information and business run. Due to the hierarchical nature of most IT security systems, there needs to be a 'God' administrator at the top of the hierarchy. These top-level privileges are tightly controlled by Cloud vendors, and normally adhere to rigorous standards of auditability and control.

Standard Cloud supply contracts respect the privacy of your information, and there should be tight controls over who can access your information, and under what circumstances.

On some foreign legal jurisdictions, Government agencies are able to demand access to your system. Examples of this are USA Patriot Act (2001) for systems hosted in the USA, or hosted outside where a US company has a financial interest in that organisation.

What happened if the Cloud provider goes out of business?

Some say that there are only two certainties in life: Death and Tax. A possible third is that: Companies do not last forever.

Markets are uncertain, and there are no absolute guarantees that the Cloud service provider of today will continue to operate in its current form unchanged over an extended timeframe.

Vendors may fail and cease operating, in which case the consumers of the vendor's Cloud computing will cease to have access to their systems, unless proven recovery and continuity strategies are put in place.

Risk: The less obvious questions

There are a number of other, no less important risks that are possibly not as obvious, which, if not surfaced for scrutiny before leaping into the Cloud, could compromise the desired outcomes, introduce unplanned cost, present hard-stop technical limitations and limit functionality.

Other questions that need to be asked are:

Is it possible to implement an Escrow arrangement in case the vendor folds?

Traditionally, for on-premises applications, the ultimate protection for an organisation from the demise of its software vendor is software *Escrow*.

* Should the vendor go out of business, your organisations' rights under Escrow allow you to immediately access and retrieve all source code, software keys and related proprietary items from the Escrow provider, and continue normal and uninterrupted operation. At that point they become self-sufficient.

Depending on the individual Cloud provider's infrastructure, it may not be possible to implement an Escrow mechanism.

* Some providers are offering a limited 'step-in' guarantee, in which case there is some protection. This depends also on the design and architecture of the vendors' infrastructure

- This may be not that practical if your data resides in three separate countries in three separate legal jurisdictions!

What are the disaster recovery implications for Cloud computing

This question is not as trivial as it may appear. Major natural disasters do occur, and you should satisfy yourself that the Cloud provider has a geographically diverse, multi-path and fully resilient Cloud infrastructure.

Are there any change control problems or issues that I should know about?

If your organisation needs to manage Cloud systems in conjunction with your on-premises systems, some Cloud providers may not comply with rigorous software development change control processes.

It is accepted 'best practice' in IT change control that a snapshot / backup of your system is taken before an upgrade, as a failback point in the event that the upgrade fails. Should this occur, your IT team need to be able to immediately access the backup data and restore the system to the pre-upgrade state, in minutes or hours.

Some Cloud providers may not provide a 'point in time' backup of your system at a time of your choosing, and you may experience lengthy delays in retrieving your backup data which is a real 'show-stopper' from a risk and governance perspective.

Change control, rollback and disaster recovery processes are invariably a focus from external auditors who need to validate that IT general controls are acceptable to either the prevailing prudential regulatory standards or specific legislative standards, such as the *Sarbanes–Oxley Act of 2002 (USA)*.

The risk and governance implications of managing multiple systems were covered in some detail in Chapter 3.

Can you collect your system at the end of the contract?

The technical complexity associated with Cloud infrastructure may physically prevent your organisation from transferring the applications to another provider, or onto your own premises.

- At contract end (or at any time, for that matter) you can extract your *data*, however you **may** *not be able to extract the application software that contains the business logic*.

- This is *as critical as the data itself*, as it this application software that defines the system itself.

Organisations that ignore or downplay the real technical and governance risks do so at their own peril, especially if integration between the Cloud and other systems (be they on-premises or other Clouds) is a core part of their strategy.

Other factors influencing risk.

Other factors that affect the risk of the implementation are:

Absence of a Cloud computing policy

Implementing a commercially sensible, Cloud computing policy mitigates against the risk of the *viral* Cloud in your organisation.

- A Viral Cloud is one which starts in a corner of the organisation, funded by local discretionary budgets, usually bypassing normal IT procurement / capital investment criteria, then grows gradually with the addition of new users. Funded, once again, from local discretionary budgets.

The importance of defining Cloud policies and accountabilities for your organisation cannot be understated. Effective internal governance is important to prevent the viral, uncontrolled and unapproved implementation of Cloud applications.

- The Cloud policy should clearly articulate the controls and accountabilities for the approval, purchase, implementation and use of *any* Cloud applications, no matter how small or trivial. Chapter 4 covered this in more detail

- The risks of an uncontrolled, viral Cloud deployment in your organisation could be significant.

Chapter 10 discusses the Cloud policy implications in multinational organisations in more detail.

Risk of unexpected costs

Some vendors are not always totally transparent on their cost models, exposing only the most acceptable cost profile to customers, for a given initial usage profile, to secure you as a customer.

Depending on the pricing policies of the Cloud vendor, additional costs could be incurred if there is a:

- Change in your user patterns. One example could be the decision to allow the system to be accessed by your customers or the public. These need to be known up front with certainty.

- Change in the relative proportion of the various types of users (e.g. regular vs. occasional users).

If the initial cost exposure of your SaaS system is small, be aware of the potential for further expansion of the system, either within your organisation or to also include customers, the public. To illustrate this point, consider the following scenario.

Scenario:

500 staff within your organisation are successfully using your Cloud system.

- The Cloud vendor has launched a new feature that will be of benefit to your customers, and enhance your customer retention prospects not to mention being a differentiator in the market when compared to your competitors for attracting new customers

- Your have potentially 5,000 named users across all of your customers who would access this system, the majority only once or twice a month

- Your Cloud license agreement states that, under the licensing arrangements from your Cloud provider, the monthly per user subscription cost is *per named user*, irrespective of how many times they access the system

- On that basis your software costs are likely to increase ten fold.

Question: How would you manage this?

This raises the concept of **concurrent use vs. named use subscription**, which was discussed in more detail in Chapter 7.

Cost may also vary depending on the type of application deployed, whether developed by you on the Cloud provider's platform, or by a third party. This was also discussed in Chapter 7.

Aligning risk appetite with the Cloud

Attempt to align your organisation's risk profile and risk appetite with that of the Cloud solution.

- If your organisation deals with critical information on which peoples lives depend or the national interest is protected or served, you may want to consider your Cloud options more carefully, by completing a rigorous and exhaustive due diligence

- If your organisation manages information that is of a more general, commercial nature, the exposure of which to external parties may not threaten the viability of your organisation, you may adopt a more relaxed risk position when considering a move to the Cloud

* * *

The takeaway messages from this chapter are:

- Know all the risks associated with the Cloud with clarity at all levels. The risks include cost certainty, technical, governance, security, performance and availability

- Due to the rapid change in the Cloud computing environment, review your risks on a more frequent basis if needed

- No less important are the commercial risks associated with vendor lock-in, forward price protection, foreign exchange exposure, vendor viability and Escrow

- Seek appropriate non-performance penalties from your Cloud provider that are representative of the true cost to your organisation from such non-performance. If this cannot be done, seek business continuity insurance, if available. Penalties should not be limited to the value of the software subscription if it is critical to your operation

- Define your Cloud project perimeter precisely. Implement clearly defined and articulated Cloud policies to prevent unauthorised viral growth of Cloud applications.

* * *

* * *

Chapter Nine

* * *

The problem of today = the solution and opportunity of tomorrow

As with the adoption of most new technologies, you need to assess whether the advantages of being an early adopter out-weigh the risks, or are you better off adopting a more cautious, wait-and-see approach? Will your organisation lose competitive advantage by delaying the adoption of this new technology?

Gartner™ predicts Cloud computing as being between two to five years from mainstream adoption. During this time, Cloud technologies will continue to develop and evolve at a fast pace.

This means that the current limitations and shortcomings of Cloud computing are largely expected to be resolved as the technology and provider's offerings continue to evolve and mature.

Speed and the evolution of Cloud computing

Globally, there are large investments being made in Cloud technologies. Analysts predict that the Worldwide Cloud computing market is expected to exceed $25 Billion by the end of 2013. With this investment comes increased:

- Capability

- Assurance

- Security

- Scalability

- Maturity, and

- Longevity.

The competitive nature of Cloud service providers will ensure that the technology matures in all directions. Implicit in this competition is the fact that some providers will cease to exist, while new, innovative entrants will appear with increasingly compelling market offerings.

Early adopter's advantage

For the astute, and well informed, there are distinct advantages from being an early adopter, primarily by being able to exploit the advantages of new and innovative technologies. This may result in a raft of benefits including lower cost, faster implementations, increased ease of use, greater reliability and less complexity.

Conversely, in the absence of rigorous due-diligence, the early and aggressive adoption of an emerging technology such as Cloud computing may result in higher than planned costs, unexpected risks and governance challenges, which in turn could adversely impact the organisation.

Fast follower's advantage

In time, the accumulated learning's from experiences of the early adopters, both customers and vendors alike, will drive the technology towards a maturity level that will satisfy the most rigorous and risk averse organisations.

The challenge for the fast followers is to obtain objective information on 'what went wrong' with the failures amongst the early adopters.

• Vendors and organisations alike are unlikely to publically announce their failed Cloud projects as this may adversely impact their organisations, whether that be in the form of financial performance, adverse publicity, brand damage or stock price.

• This fact alone skews the perceptions in the open market that Cloud technologies are easier to implement and manage than they might actually be.

The penalties of switching Cloud vendors

As there are no universally accepted standards for the interchange of data and software programs between Cloud providers (and there may never be common standards), there is always likely to be a barrier in transferring from one Cloud environment to another system, whether that be on-premises or another Cloud.

Depending on the specific nature of your industry and your organisation, this barrier could include all or some of these factors:

• Cost

• Technical complexity

• Time taken to migrate, and

• Legal or governance issues.

Utility computing and the electricity grid analogy: Partly true?

Utility computing is based, in simplest terms, on your organisation accessing a *baseline, common system* that is provided to many other organisations.

Proponents of the Cloud computing utility model suggest that, in time, organisations will eventually be accessing the majority of their IT systems by utility providers, and pay only for what they actually use.

Figure 13: 'Utility' Cloud computing has been compared to the electricity grid

- The electricity grid, water utility, or other utility provider guarantees painless provider interoperability for the consumer of these utility services. At the national level, electricity is delivered to a uniform standard[6] . Providers all have to comply with this common standard before they are able to sell their products on the market. As a consumer, switching provider is a simple exercise.

- The Cloud computing industry has, thus far, no universally accepted Cloud interoperability standards, and therefore does not, strictly speaking, fit into the 'commodity' model.

  ○ If your organisation needs to *reprogram* your core Cloud system (i.e. not make a *configuration* change) to meet your specific needs, it is no longer universally uniform, as it is then a unique variant from the base, common system

  ○ If your Cloud system cannot meet the business require-ments, you are then likely to buy or build complimen-tary systems that possibly interface with your Cloud system. The Cloud 'system' is now a *component* of your overall system

Switching from one Cloud provider to another is not a painless or trivial exercise as:

  ○ You may need to re-write the majority, if not all of your software modifications in the new system. Your old pro-grams are left behind on the outgoing Cloud

  ○ You may need to re-configure or re-build any system to system interfaces from scratch

  ○ Your database definitions may not be the same between systems, meaning that you would need to develop (or buy) data conversion programs that will transform the data to meet the data definitions of the new system.

––––––––––––––––––––

6 There are, however, exceptions to this. Eastern Japan operates 50Hertz, whereas western Japan operates 60Herts.

- ° 'You pay for what you use', is not strictly true in some Cloud providers subscription pricing models.

- ° The 'per user per month' pricing model licenses you for the number of light bulbs in your house, whether you switch them all on, or some, some of the time. If the utility computing model were to be strictly applied, you would be charges for the *actual* resources used (CPU, storage, bandwidth, etc. or any combination thereof). Chapter 7 covered this in greater detail.

Time will heal the wounds of early adopters

The evolution of the market will come with the maturity of the technology, governance models, legal and statutory frameworks, as well as improved understanding by all parties as to the underlying value, relevance and applicability of Cloud technologies.

- An immediate positive by-product of this maturation process will be the delivery of effective and elegant solutions to address the technical, governance and risk problems of today's Cloud offerings. In essence, time will largely heal the current technical and governance limitations

- The emergence of effective mechanisms that provide escrow-like protection should mitigate the risks associated with a Cloud service provider going out of business

- If, however, your current vendor is unable or unwilling to continually invest in their Cloud infrastructure and systems to keep up with the speed of the market, they (and therefore you) are likely to be left behind, on a potentially stagnant technology.

* * *

The takeaway messages from this chapter are:

- If you are able to use current Cloud technologies with technical workarounds, the rapid pace of maturation will most likely resolve current limitations thereby removing the need for these workarounds in the longer term

- Do not ignore the fundamentals of due diligence in assessing Cloud technologies. Fundamentals of good business practice do not change. Only the technology does

- Be acutely aware of vendor lock-in as the absence of standards will make changing vendors not a quick, easy or cheap exercise

- The Cloud 'utility' computing model is not a true analogy to the national electricity grid, as there is no universally acceptable Cloud interchange standard.

* * *

* * *

Chapter Ten

* * *

Implications for multinational and transnational corporations

Within a multinational organisation, each business' environment is likely to differ on a country by country basis. The purpose of this chapter is to illustrate some of the possible scenarios that could arise, and the potential implications of using Cloud computing in these instances.

This applies also to transnational, multi-divisional organisations, where each division or business unit services differing products, processes and markets.

Functionally, transnationals operate within a country's legal jurisdiction, whereas multinationals, of course, are subject to the legal jurisdictions of the countries in which they operate.

Each of the considerations is outlined below:

Legal considerations

If your chosen Cloud system is provided or owned by a foreign entity, this may add another potential layer of complexity to your specific implementation. Chapter 5 covered this in more detail.

Regulatory and governance considerations

Regulatory environments vary between countries. Depending on your type of industry, as an example, you will be subject to the industry or regulatory standards applicable to the countries in which you have a presence.

One example of this is the differing statutory requirements on minimum record retention periods for certain types of information (e.g. invoices, contract information, information subject to Freedom of Information (FOI) mandates, to name a few). How will you manage these varying requirements?

Policy settings on Cloud computing

Businesses with good IT governance frameworks will have a policy on Cloud computing. Depending on the level at which the policy on Cloud computing is set, this will have a direct bearing on your subsidiary's approach to Cloud computing.

For example, if your overseas parent organisation has a global Cloud computing policy, what implications will that policy have for your business? There are a number of possible combinations of policy settings, which may have varying degrees of impacts on your organisation, some of which are explored below:

Factor	Parent Company	Subsidiary	Some issues and questions
Cloud policy set by ...	✗	✔	What are the implications for your existing implementation if the parent mandates a Cloud policy at a future date? Can you assist in the formulation of the Cloud policies, given your experiences do date?
	✔	✗	Do you have any influence over the global policy? Can you negotiate local variations to meet your specific legal or regulatory requirements? If not, how will you resolve this?
System selection mandated by ...	✔	✗	What impact will the mandate have on your business? Does it extend to all systems offered by the mandated vendor? How can you specify higher SLAs than those mandated by the parent company if needed? How will you handle exceptions mandated by your national privacy legislation, for example?
	✗	✔	In the event of a global policy being signed, will your contract be extinguished or amended? What are the implications for your business should this occur?
Pricing of subscription set by	✔	✗	How can you negotiate competitive professional or other services fees with the vendor if you have no buying power? What happens if the local vendor offers a lower price than the global contracted price? Who covers foreign exchange gains/losses?
	✗	✔	Are there missed opportunities from global buying power?

Table 2: Influence on Cloud policy settings in multinational organisations

Common Cloud system does not equal common standards

Even though there may be a common system used across a multinational organisation, this may be in name only. Unless the organisation is globally uniform in its systems, technology, business processes, data standards and naming conventions, local instances of the systems will invariably exist.

Differing data structures, naming and number conventions

In the absence of global mandates, local subsidiaries may determine their own product number and naming conventions. Should this be the case, this may have implications in the event of any data exchanges or data consolidation between organisations and the parent entity at a later date. If, for example, each subsidiary implemented a local, non-standard general ledger, financial consolidation of data across subsidiaries would be inefficient when compared to the adoption of globally consistent standards.

Differing system configurations

Even though subsidiaries may have the same system from the same vendor, and using the same data and naming conventions, the configuration *and implementation* of the system could be different in each case to meet local business processing needs. This could have implications for the interpretation of standard reports, for example.

Internet speeds or reliability

Internet speeds are a problem in some developing countries[7], and could adversely impact the use of Cloud computing systems in those instances. If your business runs very time sensitive processes, the Internet performance in both bandwidth (carrying capacity) as well as latency (speed) need to be investigated and tested.

No need for IT infrastructure in remote offices

One of the benefits inherent in Cloud technology (public or private) is that high value applications can be delivered to users anywhere that the Internet can be accessed, avoiding the

---

7   And even in some developed countries, in regional areas, where Internet services are non-existent or slow.

need for IT infrastructure (e.g. servers, data centres, etc.) in (developing) countries and regions that would have problems supporting the infrastructure locally. The ability to quickly setup or relocate international offices is significantly enhanced if no on-premises IT infrastructure is required.

Mobility

For highly mobile managers and staff, Cloud systems are accessible from anywhere, which presents its own advantages in that there is a standard user interface to the Cloud systems, irrespective of location.

Globally mobile staff and managers are increasingly able to access your Cloud systems from their handheld devices. In some instances, this may reduce the need for dedicated desktops and laptops, further lowering IT infrastructure and support costs to your organisation.

* * *

The takeaway messages from this chapter are:

* Multinational organisations will be potentially subject to multi-jurisdictional legislative and regulatory issues, and should develop mechanisms of avoiding policy conflicts

* Cloud can simplify the effort, and lower the costs associated with the setup of a new branch office, provided minimum acceptable Internet speed and coverage standards are met

* For pervasive access to Cloud technologies, ensure all your users have access to high speed and reliable Internet connections.

* * *

* * *

Chapter Eleven

* * *

Suitability for Cloud: What's your business environment?

There are a number of factors that will determine how easy it will be for you to implement a new Cloud enterprise system in your organisation. If all of the following statements are TRUE, then you should be able to progress relatively swiftly through your journey to Cloud computing:

- Your Cloud system is standalone. (i.e. you do not need to build any system interfaces)

- You will not need to write software programs. (i.e. changes are made using configuration screens)

- Your data in the Cloud is not highly sensitive (e.g. Government security clearance)

- If the vendor goes out of business (and you are unable to access your system) you have a workaround in place

- You do not have to commit to any long-term costs

- Any write-off costs associated with moving from any existing systems are not material

- User training on the new system is likely to be easy and/or intuitive

- There are no material exit costs or technical restraints when you do wish to exit the Cloud system at a point in the future

- There are no significant governance issues that concern you about the new system.

However, *your organisation's stage of maturity and business environment* also plays an important part in the relevance and selection of Cloud computing. Some of these factors are outlined below.

How proprietary are your current systems?

Customised and heavily modified systems

The greater the complexity of your existing on-premises systems, the less likely they are easily transferrable to the Cloud. Complex on-premises systems invariably contain a large amount of custom written software that fits your specific business requirements.

Specialised bespoke (customised for your specific requirements) systems such as complex billing, order processing, accounting, leasing management systems or specialised forecasting systems are unlikely to be easily transferred to the Cloud. It is also unlikely that niche, highly bespoke applications are going to be available in the Public Cloud market whilst the market is still maturing.

If you do find a Cloud provider whose system is a close fit to your requirements, do not underestimate the time, effort and inherent complexity of the software development process should you need to undertake major programming enhancements.

Some providers (such as Salesforce™) encourage customers to write their customised applications on their Cloud infrastructure.

The primary risk of investing heavily in time, effort and cost in the development of bespoke systems in the Cloud provider's infrastructure is the fact that you are unlikely to be able to extract those programs and associated business logic should you wish to switch providers at some future point.

To illustrate this point, consider the following simplified scenario:

Scenario:

• You run a publicly listed company that provides specialised financial products and services which depend on IT systems which require a high degree of customisation, to be able to differentiate yourself from the competition. You have a five year planning horizon. There are no 'off the shelf' Cloud systems that meet your requirements, the closest is approximately a 70% fit to your current requirements. You have the option of moving your applications to the Cloud, as you have been told that it will be a lot cheaper.

Assessment:

• There are no 'off the shelf' systems that meet your requirements, so extensive programming changes are required. Given the degree of customisation, you will be making significant investments in internal development of these applications, irrespective where they actually reside. Should you wish to, at a later date, switch Cloud providers, you most likely will need to re-write all your programs in the new supplier's system.

Recommendation:

• On-premises is the likely alternative due to the certainty of cost, and full control over the IT environment, not to mention potential governance and legislative considerations.

Standardised, 'commodity' systems

'Commodity' systems, on the other hand, are more likely to be contenders for Cloud computing. Examples of these systems include email, network file storage or generic websites. As a user, you have no need to program anything. You just use the system 'as-is', and configure the system to meet your requirements.

To illustrate this point, consider the following simplified scenario:

Scenario:

• You run a company, whose email system is somewhat outdated, underperforming, and not meeting all of your current business requirements. It is due for a upgrade or replacement. You have also confirmed that there are no global policy mandates on which email system you should use.

Assessment:

• All you require is a stable, cost effective, and easy to use email system, so you are considering a Cloud based email solution as a replacement for your on-premises email system. You have completed a five year total cost of ownership analysis, and compared this to the projected cost of an equivalent on-premises system. Cloud is cheaper. Risks are acceptable. There are no significant governance problems.

Recommendation:

• Cloud is the likely preferred option due to the certainty of a lower total cost, avoidance of the need to employ specialist technical staff, and assurance that the email system will be continually upgraded as new features are made available.

What is the likely life expectancy of the system?

The expected life span of the system will have a bearing on the Total Cost of Ownership (TCO) of the system. Ostensibly, a perpetual subscription model implies a perpetual cost. This is in contrast to the buy-and-depreciate software model, where past a certain point in time the costs of subscription may exceed the buy-and-depreciate software model.

Chapter 7 covered this in more detail.

To illustrate this point, consider the following simplified scenario:

Scenario:

•   You need to replace your outdated system, however you are planning to sell your business in 12 months, to realise the capital gain of the organisation, and invest in other business ventures. Your business does not need any special, proprietary systems – all you need are standard accounting, order entry, customer service and inventory systems.

Assessment:

•   The TCO horizon is 12 months, so provided that the total cost of the Cloud system is less than the total cost of the on-premises equivalent, select Cloud

•   You may find that the saleable value of the business is likely to be higher as the prospective buyer will not need to take possession of physical assets such as data centres, servers etc.

•   It is also more likely that you are able to implement the Cloud system sooner rather than the on-premises system.

Recommendation:

- Cloud is likely to be the preferred option.

Lack of finance

If your organisation is unable to secure capital or finance with which to purchase either IT infrastructure or enterprise on-premises software licenses, you may have no alternative but to choose Cloud computing.

There are a number of finance related considerations, these being:

- **Funding IT from cash flow alone**

You may adopt a specific policy of only funding investments in IT systems from cash flow, in which case Cloud is the viable option, where you have the ability to expand or scale back your systems to suit your business cycles.

- **Eliminating the possibility of write-offs**

You may wish to keep all your IT costs off balance sheet, thereby eliminating the possibility of software and hardware write-offs. Also, Cloud computing avoids the risk of maintenance contract early penalty charges.

Uncertainty over the number of system users over time

Should the number of users vary considerable over the lifespan of the system, this may have a significant impact on the TCO, depending on the type of licensing model your Cloud provider is offering.

To illustrate this, consider the following possible life cycle:

- Proof of Concept (POC) trial – 50 users

- End Year 1 (All employees) – 500 users

- End of year 3 (All customers) – 10,000 users

- End of year 4 (Public access) – 100,000+users

It is imperative that you obtain a clear understanding of the expected number of users over the life of the Cloud system.

Chapter 7 discussed the importance of named user, concurrent user and server based license models on the cost of Cloud systems for varying numbers of users.

Scenario:

- You run a not-for-profit organisation delivering home based and community care services. 90% of your users are mobile and need basic CRM functionality – in fact they only need to update activities such as client visit details, after each visit.

Assessment :

- SaaS CRM systems provide far more features than would be used, so presents an expensive option. Also the number of concurrent users is low, while the number of named users is high. Your intended Cloud provider charges you subscription costs on the basis of named users, rather than concurrent user.

Recommendation:

- On premises is likely to the winner due to cost certainty and low per user system utilisation.

In summary, in addition to the cost, governance and risk factors, you should also be considering your organisation's stage of maturity and specific business environment, as these also plays an important part in the relevance of Cloud computing to your organisation.

* * *

The takeaway messages from this chapter are:

- Highly proprietary on-premises IT systems are less likely to be easily migrated to the Cloud

- 'Commodity' systems such as email and file storage are more likely to be candidates for Cloud

- The life expectancy of your system plays a part in assessing the total cost of ownership. Be aware of any equivalent on-premises breakeven point, beyond which Cloud may be more expensive

- Include considerations of your business' environment and stage of evolution in Cloud decisions

- Finance restrictions and caveats may lead you towards Cloud

- Be aware of the volatility in your expected number of system users, and cost these scenarios into your Cloud cost modelling.

* * *

* * *

Chapter Twelve

* * *

Implications for governance

Good governance is the accepted norm for organisations, and underpins the consistency of quality, management of risk and seeks to offer assurances over the long term viability of your organisation. Governance standards and statutory mandates vary over time, and an important aspect of any enterprise IT system, is that the system is able to meet future governance and statutory requirements.

Governance and standards frameworks have been around for a long time, and are represented in a large number of standards, frameworks and variants thereof, such as:

*   ISO 20000 and ITIL (IT service management)

*   ISO 9000 (quality)

*   ISO 14001 (environment)

*   ISO 27001 (information and risk)

*   Six Sigma (operational performance and defect identification)

*   COBIT (information assurance)

- Balanced Scorecard (measuring a company's activities)

- Prince2 and PMBOK (projects), and

- SOX / JSOX (business auditing and control).

Additionally, there are the statutory and regulatory require-ments, which vary according to country, legal jurisdiction, in-dustry, services delivered by your organisation as well as types of products sold. Examples include the following Australian Commonwealth Government acts:

- The Privacy Act 1988

- Corporations Act 2001

- Competition and Consumer Act 2010.

To a certain degree, these regulatory and governance frame-works often define *how* your organisation runs itself.

What are the key governance questions you need to ask?

Some of the governance related questions that should be considered in the assessment of Cloud computing includes:

- If you can implement a Cloud system very rapidly, can you change your business processes, user documentation and user policies at the same speed? Ensuring that associated business processes and business related governance frame-works are constantly aligned with the operation of the Cloud system may not be a trivial task, especially if constant configuration changes are permitted, that alter the perfor-mance of the system

- How familiar are your regulators and/or auditors with the concepts and governance issues surrounding Cloud computing?

- What are the implications of any enterprise governance policies? For example, do you have a Cloud computing *governance* policy? (If not, maybe its time to think about one)

- How will you adapt your governance frameworks to meet significantly different approaches to the implementation of Cloud based enterprise systems, whether they are on-premises, hosted, Public Cloud, Private Cloud, hybrid Cloud, or any combination thereof?

- Do your regulators offer any guidelines for the adoption of Cloud technology? These may be very helpful and reduce your effort in ensuring ongoing compliance to the prevailing regulations and standards

- Not all the risks inherent in the emerging Public Cloud technologies are well or equally understood across organisations, whether they be commercial, legal, security or governance. Do you know everything there is to know that is relevant to your minimum statutory and governance frameworks as they relate to Cloud computing?

What are some of the project management issues in Cloud computing?

The Project Management Office (PMO) is charged with the timely and cost effective delivery of projects for most organisations. The conventional approach to enterprise projects may need to be reviewed for rapid deployment. If your organisation's PMO operates to accepted standards such as Prince2™, how do you need to change your framework in the light of Cloud computing?

Consider the following influences and factors:

a) Reversal of the traditional business case, that is: *'buy* before you *try'*

   o Cloud offers, potentially, enterprise ready applications in hours or days, and when combined with easy to manage configuration options, there is likely to be less tolerance by impatient business stakeholders to suffer 'paralysis by analysis' associated with the requirements gathering and analysis phases

   o 'Better 90% on time, than late and perfect' is often the catch-cry of business stakeholders who are becoming increasingly impatient with the complexity and lead times on IT projects

   o What form will your business case take if you are not able to identify the total cost exposure at the start of the project? Are the benefits based on opinions or can they be substantiated in evidence?

b) In relation to projects supported by Cloud technologies, and with specific reference to the *pilot project to production scale-up phases:*

   o What pressure will there be to relax the cost assessment exercise and merely scale up to production if the pilot project is successful, especially if the system is extremely popular with the business? Chapter 2 covered this in more detail.

c) Project risk mitigation strategies:

○ Not all the risks inherent in the emerging Cloud technologies may be well understood by organisations, whether they be commercial, legal, security, governance or availability related

○ Some of these risks cover change management and rollback provisioning, which are at the heart of good project and IT governance, and depend on the technical capabilities of specific Cloud systems.

d) Problems associated with managing Cloud project boundary conditions:

○ With the increasing availability of development tools, as well as vendor 'applications markets', there are a large array of third party applications written on the Cloud vendors infrastructure, the quality of which may be variable. The Salesforce™ App Exchange, Android™ Market and the Apple iStore™ are examples of such eco-systems

○ Some of these applications can be implemented by ends users, and may extend the boundary of projects in an uncontrolled manner.

e) Highlight some of the challenges in approach to the implementation of enterprise Cloud projects using methodologies such as Prince2™

○ The comprehensive use of rigorous, large scale project methodologies such as Prince2™ are often not appropriate for all but the largest of enterprise IT projects, although selected elements are universally applicable to all projects

○ The interpretation and adaptation of the various large scale project methodologies to volatile 'implement first and modify as you go' environments needs some careful consideration.

* * *

The takeaway messages from this chapter are:

- Identify which statutory and regulatory frameworks are impacted by the potential implementation of Cloud computing, and what these impacts are likely to be

- Be aware of the potential changes that need to be implemented in your existing governance frameworks, to ensure continued compliance to the applicable standards

- Ensure that your Project Management Office (PMO) is aware of the potential impacts of Cloud computing for implementation initiatives.

* * *

* * *

Chapter Thirteen

* * *

The promise of the imminent future

The relentless development of new and innovative IT Technologies presents ongoing opportunities within your organisation for increased revenue, productivity, value and flexibility at potentially a lower Total Cost of Ownership (TCO).

Cloud is no exception to this. With the Cloud being at the peak of the Gartner™ Hype-Cycle, organisations looking to take advantage of the real benefits of Cloud technology should ensure that their due diligence effort matches the potential cost and risk exposure of your organisation.

- Essentially, if you have a medium to high risk appetite and the majority of your organisation's revenue does not hinge on the decision, then a more relaxed position can be adopted in this decision making process. Conversely, if the costs and risks are high, proportionate amount of due diligence effort should be applied.

Cloud facilitating innovation

As outlined in Chapter 3, organisations that wish to support or drive innovation initiatives, may find that Cloud computing is an excellent way of facilitating this innovation.

Cloud technologies are generally a good fit for rapid startup, small pilot projects. The walk-away costs are minimised, should the innovation fail.

Cloud for the desktop

The presence on the market of word processing, spreadsheet and other typical desktop productivity software available from the Cloud (e.g. Microsoft Office 365™ and Google Apps™) is very compelling in that:

- The majority of PCs and Laptops have a full suite of software, which is often underutilised. It makes more sense to pay for what is actually used

- You need not spend time and effort reconciling actual PC license software license usages to your entitlements. Cloud based entitlements are always compliant, by their very nature

- Your organisation does not need to provision and support standardised PCs and laptops to staff – as long as they can access the Internet by a browser they can run their documents, spreadsheets, etc.

- Your organisation can move towards a 'bring your own' (BYO) computer policy, when and where it makes sense. Users can bring device of their choosing (iPad™, PC, laptop, Tablet, etc), This further saves on internal PC support, and working capital in providing PC's and laptops for all staff

- No internal IT infrastructure is needed to support these desktop Cloud applications other than an Internet connection

- Real-time collaboration between people working with documents, spreadsheets and the like is possible in Cloud desktop applications

- Purchase of client PC software licenses is not required, releasing working capital for other purposes.

Stick to the fundamentals

The fundamentals of running and managing organisations have remained unchanged for many years. Cloud technology, as with any other innovation, has the potential to do things cheaper, faster and better.

To achieve these benefits you need to:

- Know the true cost

- Know the value

- Know the risk

- Know when to buy

- Know what to buy, and

- Know when to exit the technology and/or upgrade.

This essentially means that you need to know what *questions* to ask stakeholders such as suppliers, your management, your staff, your customers, your lawyers, your business partners, your regulators, and most importantly *yourself* about the realisable value in deploying Cloud technologies.

If you know what question to ask, you are in a position to assess the relevance and importance of the answer. This in turn, reduces uncertainty and maximises the probability of achieving the stated objectives in the deployment and use of Cloud computing, the latest IT paradigm.

Go forth and explore the possibilities in knowledge and confidence!

* * *

Chapter Fourteen

The Cloud Assessment Framework

It is in your best interests, as a consumer of Cloud technologies, that all relevant risk, cost and governance aspects of Cloud computing are exposed, and openly and independently discussed *as they apply to your organisation's specific situation*. At the heart of this process is knowing what questions to ask.

There are real benefits to be realised in the implementation of Cloud computing, however these can be offset by adverse influences that would otherwise have been identified in a rigorous due diligence process.

You know the upside with precision. What about the possible downsides?

Ideally, you will already be able to assess the upside potential and value of Cloud computing to your organisation. By the time you are considering factors such as cost and governance in any level of detail, you are most likely already part way down the sourcing and procurement path.

- The risk to your organisation lies not in only identifying the upside potential for Cloud computing, *but in exposing*

117

unexpected cost, risk, operational or other governance challenges that could have been otherwise identified <u>up front</u> by improved due diligence.

Part of the challenge in assessing new or emerging technologies such as Cloud computing is to know:

- What questions to ask on which aspects of Cloud

- How to ask these questions

- To whom they should be directed

- The relevance and relative importance of each question for *your business*, and

- To know when you are provided an answer that is either incomplete or of questionable integrity.

The Cloud Assessment Framework – just a suggestion

The Cloud Assessment Framework in this book consists of a series of 'plain English' questions that need to be asked of the various stakeholders to gain a comprehensive assessment of the *risk, cost and governance issues of the SaaS Cloud* at any stage of the process.

The heart of the framework in this book is the inventory of questions. The framework itself is only offered as one possible approach to conducting an assessment. You may wish to adapt this to your own internal governance and assessment processes.

- You may be looking at Cloud for the first time, expanding your pilot project, or looking to reconfigure your existing Cloud system in a different way. This framework applies to all scenarios

118

- The framework is independent of any specific technology, and does not assume that there are solutions or remedies to address any of your concerns. There may or may not be cost effective, elegant solutions to any specific technical or governance issue, however it is important that you are able to satisfy *yourself* that the solutions offered are acceptable to you with known:

  - Cost

  - Performance capabilities

  - Risk

  - Governance standards, and

  - Applicability for its intended purpose.

Not all the questions are specific to Cloud technologies, but need to be asked irrespective, as they have a direct bearing on the outcomes of your Cloud project.

Each question is not of equal importance. Only *you* will be able to determine the relative importance or even relevance of a particular question as it applies to *your specific project, Business Unit or whole organisation*.

The relevance of each question may well vary for each project, however it is recommended that should a question be deleted from your review, you nevertheless satisfy yourself that there are no adverse factors that could have been identified that may have a bearing on you achieving your intended outcomes.

Request for Tender (RFT) / Request for Quote (RFQ)

This framework may be useful for organisations seeking to publish a Request for Tender / Proposal (RFT / RFP) to a range of

Cloud vendors. You may wish to include some of these questions, into any of your RFP/RFT documentation, suitably modified for your particular purpose.

Because a vendor has ticked a 'we comply' checkbox for a specific factor, is not necessarily a guarantee that the requirements will be fully met and satisfied. Seek evidence.

How to use the Framework

The questions are grouped into categories, which include areas such as:

- Change control

- Compliance

- Contract end

- Innovation

- IT Staff

- Legal

- Multinational

- Requirements, and

- Risk.

Treat the existing categories as indicative only. The most important factor is the specific question itself. Some questions can cover multiple categories.

- For example, the question "Will your organisation need to exchange data between the Cloud and multiple other systems?" can be categorised as both IT and Business functions, as the integration may occur at the infrastructure or application layers.

* * *

The Questions:

Each question is posed with the specific purpose of making you aware of the individual factor.

> Think of each question as analogous to switching on a Christmas tree light, one at a time, in a darkened room. After a while, the true shape of the tree becomes clear.

Some questions may appear trivial or obvious at first, however on deeper investigation, the complexity may be exposed. Once again, this complexity may be evident in some projects, and not others. The key variable is *your specific* situation.

Only *you* can assess the relevance of each question to your project, organisation or business unit.

The Rationale:

Each question has a suggested rationale. This rationale provides additional contextual information that may be either a statement of intent or offering clarification, or both.

The rationale may also offer additional questions, the sole purpose of which is to invite you to explore the issue further.

The stakeholders:

There are a number of potential stakeholders associated with each question and may include, but are not necessarily limited to:

- CEO
- CFO
- CIO
- COO
- HR
- Executive Management Team
- Risk Manager
- IT - Technical
- Global Governance
- Auditor
- Legal Council
- Statutory and Regulatory Agencies
- Channel and Business Partners
- Clients and Customers
- Dealers / Franchises
- Consultants / System integrators.

Your specific industry and organisation would no doubt have differing stakeholder categories. Itemise these as you see fit for your organisation and industry.

What part does each stakeholder play in answering each question?

Given that the questions cover a range of topics, each stakeholder will need to be involved in some or all of these questions in one form or another.

In order to match how each question relates to each relevant stakeholder, four categories of involvement are suggested, for each question / issue, these being:

Responsibility – (R)

Having responsibility for doing the work associated with the question. There is typically only one role with a participation type of Responsible.

Accountability – (A)

Being ultimately answerable for the issue in question. There can be only one person accountable for each item.

Consulted - (C)

Those whose opinions are sought, typically subject matter experts.

Informed – (I)

Kept up-to-date on progress, usually in the form of a one-way communication.

In this way, the relevance of each stakeholder is appropriately matched to the specific issue or question, and ensures that all stakeholders are involved only as needed.

Next steps

The following table illustrates the layout of the framework, in tabular format:

Question	Rationale	Stakeholders					
		CEO	CIO	CFP	HR	Legal	Audit
Question 1	Rationale 1	I	R	A	C	-	C
Question 2	Rationale 2	C	I	-	R	A	I
Question 3	Rationale 3	-	R	A	I	C	C
Question 4	Rationale 4	A	R	C	-	-	I

<u>Table 3:</u> Cloud Assessment – Stakeholder framework

It is up to your organisation to complete this table by taking each question, together with its rationale, and then identifying:

1. Which two stakeholders need to be assigned Responsibility (R) and Accountability (A) and

2. Which of the remaining stakeholders need to be Consulted (C) or Informed (I)?

The following steps suggest how you could implement this framework for *your* specific Cloud projects.

Step 1: Identify which questions are relevant to your project or Cloud initiative. You may also wish to add other questions as you see appropriate, to meet your specific needs.

Step 2: Edit each question to suit your specific purposes, industry specific terminology or wording.

Step 3: Identify all the relevant stakeholders that are likely to be impacted by, or have an influence over the success of the project.

Step 4: For each question, assign one **R**, one **A** and as many **C**s and/or **I**s as are relevant.

Step 5: Commence the assessment, which can take many forms, including face to face meetings, online survey, workshops or focus groups. Choose the most appropriate approach for your specific situation.

Step 6: Process the result of the assessment. Once again, the specific approach will vary for each organisation and project.

Over to you

It is beyond the scope of this book to guide you on how to specifically manage the process of transforming the findings that resulted from the questioning framework, through to making a final, appropriate decision for your organisation.

You are the best equipped to now mitigate or manage the now known risks, costs and governance pitfalls.

In conclusion.....

If all you achieve from reading this book is to obtain a much clearer understanding of where the risks, costs and governance pitfalls of Cloud computing might lie, then you are in a far stronger position to:

• Proceed into the Cloud with increased certainty

• Invest in the Cloud with increased certainty

- Know your cost exposure with increased certainty

- Understand your governance limitations (if any at all) with increased certainty, and most importantly

- Achieve *your organisation's goals and objectives* with increased certainty.

Like any good pilot will tell you, when you're flying in the Cloud, as long as you know where the ground is at any time, you'll generally get to your objective.

Cloud computing has huge potential for individuals, organisations and economies alike, so look forward to the benefits of this new paradigm!

Enjoy your journey.

* * *

The Questions:

1. Architecture and solution fit

Question	Rationale
1.1 Will your business requirements be a close fit for Cloud Computing 'out of the box'?	If your requirements are highly specific and complex, and no close 'fit' exists in the Cloud computing market, they are unlikely to be a 'commodity' application, and as such, may be less likely a good candidate for Cloud computing. Extensive modifications to your Cloud application are most likely not possible, due to the standardised 'commodity' computing model.
1.2 Can you make all the changes to the Cloud system by configuring it, that is, without programming?	If the Cloud system does not require programming, changes can be implemented without deep technical IT skills, however specific skills are still required in system administration of the Cloud system as it has been implemented in your organisation.

2. Audit

Question	Rationale
2.1 What rights do you have to request an independent audit of the provider's processes and infrastructure to verify your specific regulatory or statutory compliance?	The fact that a provider has a compliance certificate to a defined standard may provide some comfort, however the scope of the specific standard may not apply to all aspects of their operation. Ask to sight the *statement of applicability* for each standard. Seek confirmation that every aspect of your system is appropriately covered by some form of independent assessment.

2.2 Will your organisation be able to inspect and review the provider's internal infrastructure and processes to satisfy your organisation (or your organisation's regulators or auditors) of the robustness of their internal management processes?	Depending on the degree of due diligence required, and your organisation's risk appetite, you may request to inspect the provider's infrastructure. Some of the larger, global providers will not permit this, so you need to reply on independent certification. Confirm with your regulators that these certification standards are appropriate and adequate.

3. Change Control

Question	Rationale
3.1 What software version and change control mechanisms exist in the Cloud?	One of the advantages of public Cloud is that you need not worry about software and infrastructure upgrades. This is an advantage, but also presents some challenges if you have interfaces between Cloud and your systems. 'Best practice' software change control processes rely on careful testing and approval processes before upgrades are implemented to live systems. If you routinely just accept any upgrades without testing, some of your system interfaces may not work properly.
3.2 Can your organisation take a 'full system backup' (including program, data, business logic, access control and identity management) of your Cloud system when it suits you?	Taking a 'snapshot' of your system (also known as a 'full system backup') is an important part of the system change control process. It is important that you can take system backups when it suits YOUR organisation, and not dependant on the provider to do this on a schedule. The provider's standard backup schedules may not suit your timing.

3.3 If your organisation is planning to making a change to a system that interfaces your on-premises systems to the Cloud, how long will it take your provider to provide you with your 'full system backup'?	If you are implementing a change to interface systems, it is usual practice to take a 'point in time' backup as a restore point in the in the event of needing to fallback to the pre-upgrade point. Imagine if your upgraded system overwrote customer address line 1 with "1 Elm Street' for all 200,000 customers. Your production database is immediately worthless, and you have to reinstate your restore-point data ASAP, typically in minutes or at most hours. If your Cloud provider cannot restore your entire system in an acceptable timeframe, this may breach your current minimum acceptable governance standards.
3.4 Irrespective of the reason, and should the need exist, what is the default 'restore-point' from which you can restore *specific elements* of your data?	Unlikely, but not impossible scenarios include a failure of your internal software change control processes (or possibly even those of the vendor!), resulting in the accidental erasure of some of your data or data corruption. In this event, what retrieval processes are involved, and at what specific point in time is the data valid? (e.g. last Thursday at 12:38:45 am, or 30 seconds ago?). They key determinant is to understand if, how and the length of time it would take to get your data back from the vendor's underlying system backup and restore processes (i.e. not specifically initiated by you).

4. Consulting

Question	Rationale
4.1 Will your organisation employ a consultant to help with the Cloud system in pre-sale, selection and implementation phases?	Reliance on a consultant may be beneficial, but be aware of any indirect alliances and preferences for specific providers, if independence of opinion and capability is important.
4.2 Is your Cloud consultant completely technology agnostic and independent of any provider?	Identify, if possible, what financial incentives your consultant derives from any provider, if any.
4.3 Does the consultant have proven expertise in the assessment of Cloud technologies in the context of your organisation?	Cloud is somewhat different to the conventional on-premises systems. They need to have proven expertise in Cloud as relevant to your organisation. Seek evidence and investigate thoroughly. Remember, each implementation is different to varying degrees.
4.4 What core expertise does your consultant have in technical, implementation, integration, financial, commercial, regulatory and governance factors?	It is important that at the end of the day, they are able to integrate all these factors into a total support capability. Technical competence is only a small part of the overall picture.
4.5 Does your consultant have a particular implementation Methodology? What is it and where is it most applicable?	Being locked into a specific methodology can be useful, however, be aware of the shortcomings in a methodology if it does not cover all your specific requirements.

4.6 Does the consultant have expertise in the particular regulatory and statutory requirements in your industry?	Your particular industry may have specific legislative, governance or client contractual requirements. If you are unable to satisfy yourself that your consultant is aware of the key issues, seek supplemental advice from, for example, your legal council, provided they have expertise in Cloud and the related issues.

5. Contract end

Question	Rationale
5.1 Can your organisation recreate various documents from a prior period after you have departed the Cloud?	Once your organisation has transitioned out of the Cloud system at some point in the future, you may have the low level data, but no easy way of interpreting the data as the applications and business logic has been left behind. (For example, recreating copies of invoices, statements). This is especially relevant if most of these 'documents' were all in electronic form. This has potentially serious implications for any Freedom of Information (FOI) legislation. Seek an alternative way of storing and retrieving documents that are subject to such legislation.
5.2 Are there any exit costs when your organisation wishes to exit the Cloud system?	If you are carrying the data and functionality forward to be run on another system at some point in the future, the costs associated with this migration may not be trivial. If you extract the data, for example, it is unlikely that it will be in exactly the format of the new system, so data conversions and reconfigurations may be needed. Are these costs material to your current decision?

Question	Rationale
5.3 What is the Contract duration for your Cloud systems?	If the contract has a defined end date, with no guarantee of a renewal on the same or more favourable terms and conditions, what risk would that present to your organisation at that point in the future? Do not underestimate the influence of vendor lock-in.
5.4 What guarantees exist that all data is destroyed at contract end?	Are you able to seek independent verification of the destruction or removal of your organisation information (including all cyclical backups, data mirrors, etc.), should it be deemed necessary?
5.5 Under what circumstances can the provider terminate your agreement 'for cause'?	If you are late paying the account or if you are under financial distress (temporary cash flow problems, voluntary receivership or administration), the provider may be entitled to sever your services without notice. Know your rights.
5.6 What are the contract transition out terms and conditions?	At what time is your system no longer available to you for data retrieval? Some providers retain your system for a maximum of 30 days (possibly in a 'read only' state) after termination. Can you extend this period?
5.7 Can you go in and collect your system at the end of the contract?	Depending on the technical design of the Cloud provider's infrastructure, you may be able to able to retrieve some of the system. Confirm exactly what you can and cannot extract on conclusion of the relationship, and in what form this will take.

Question	Rationale
5.8 Can you renew, extend successive contract(s) on the same / more favourable terms and costs?	Are you able to negotiate a perpetual contract? If not you may not be able to renegotiate a contract renewal if the then terms and conditions are not as favourable as your existing contract. This is where vendor lock-in is a potential problem.
5.9 What are the provider transition-out arrangements specified in your contract(s)?	Does the contract contain a sunset notice period, and if so what limitations does this impose? For example, if your organisation gives notice to cancel or not renew, do you have a set number of days before the Cloud system is switched off, and if you request an extension of this deadline, what are the costs? Will the vendor charge you full list price rather than your discounted price?

6. Cost

Question	Rationale
6.1 Switching to the Cloud: What are any cost write offs of any existing software, hardware being decommissioned?	Moving systems means decommissioning outgoing systems and infrastructure, and exiting any relevant contracts. These write-off costs may be material, and should form part of the business case justification.

Question	Rationale
6.2 Identify what costs (if any) are associated with the deployment of the Cloud system through handheld mobile devices (Android™, iPhone™, iPad™ etc), whether they be provided by the provider, or written by your organisation on the provider's system.	Some providers charge for the delivery of non-core applications to Smartphone's. This means that if you develop an application, or purchase a Cloud application from the third party eco-system, you may be liable for an additional cost.
6.3 What cap exists on year-on-year percentage increases in costs?	Mitigate against price gouging when your organisations' locked into a provider and they know it! For example, annual increases may be capped to the prevailing national inflation rate, CPI or other independent benchmark. If you are billed in your local currency, the provider carries the foreign exchange risk.
6.4 What does your contract say about the license costs of the various types of and categories of users?	Some providers have differing prices that depend on the type of user. Know what they are, e.g. administrators, anonymous users, named users, etc.
6.5 Are your organisation's system usage patterns likely to change much in the life of the Cloud solution? If so what cost projections / scenarios have been worked out?	As your organisation's user base grows, how will this impact the cost of your Cloud? For example, if you are planning to expand the system to your dealers, customers or the public at large, what will your costs be?

Question	Rationale
6.6 Do you know your existing IT costs by application on total? And by user?	If you are replacing existing on-premises systems with Cloud, on what basis are you comparing these costs, and over what time frame? $50/month/user may cost you $2 Million more than a $5 Million up-front license for an equivalent on-premises application over a 3 year period, and $4 Million over a 5 year period. Know your TCO (Total Cost of Ownership) exposure with certainly, unless you prefer to gamble.
6.7 Is there an on-premises (owned but hosted) vs Cloud break even point for 'own and depreciate' vs Cloud costs and when is it?	Analogous to renting vs. buying a house. At some point you will own the house, and the TCO of renting may become higher.
6.8 Can your organisation compare the Cloud and on-premises costs on a like-for-like cost basis? i.e. Per User Per Month Per Application (PUPMA)	Being able to compare 'like-for-like' costs demonstrates the true comparative cost of various alternatives. For example, how can you otherwise know for certain that $50/user/month is cheaper than a $1 Million purchase after 48 months?
6.9 Do you know how to transform your existing IT costs in total to an equivalent PUPMA basis?	PUPMA calculations require a combined knowledge of your on-premises IT architecture, all IT costs, their allocations and accounting treatments. Any assumptions as to the cost distribution of overheads need to be clearly understood.

Question	Rationale
6.10 Do you have existing hardware, software and service maintenance contracts for outgoing systems?	Once you identify all existing IT services and supply contracts that have a bearing on any decision to migrate or expand Cloud, including early termination, transitional arrangements, you will know the early termination costs associated with each of these. The write-off costs could be material. Additionally, you should identify any restrictive exit or transitional conditions that may apply during a transition-out period associated with each contract (if applicable).
6.11 Is your provider's contract explicit about the costs associated with all possible user types?	Specify the types and user categories that your organisation are likely to encounter during the life of the system (e.g. public occasional user, internal staff user, anonymous user, authenticated self-registering users, administrators, programmers, dealers, business partners, etc.). Subscription charges may vary depending on the vendor.
6.12 What license / subscription model does the Cloud provider offer?	Identify all possible subscription types, and their precise costing mechanisms. Confirm if named user, concurrent usage (largely on-premises, some Cloud), server based license (on-premises), or any other, or a combination thereof.

Question	Rationale
6.13 Do you know the usage intensity for each user of the Cloud system? (e.g. 30% of users log in once a month?)	Usage intensity is a useful measure of the effective utilisation of a system. If the cost is the same for a user that accesses the system once a month, never or 100 times per day, which represents the greatest value to your organisation?
6.14 Are you aware of possible changes to your usage loads on the system and how will these be costed?	Should you, for example, after a period of time, introduce mathematically intensive calculations into your systems (e.g. implementing a forecasting system) which results in surges in processor loads or network bandwidth, data storage etc, how will your provider mange this and what will the implications be for your organisation? Multi-tenanted Clouds have performance limits placed on each customer. What happens if you have a peak demand? Do you pay a penalty or does your system grind to a halt?

7. Drivers

Question	Rationale
7.1 Is the primary factor in considering Cloud to lower total IT cost?	Be aware of all the hidden and associated costs of implementation. Seek evidence that it is in fact cheaper by insisting on a POC (Proof of Concept) trial, and analyse your existing costs on a like for like basis. If you don't do that, how do you know with certainty that it will, in fact, be cheaper?

Question	Rationale
7.2 Is the primary determinant of considering Cloud to improve IT productivity by spending less cost, time and effort in programming your enterprise systems, and 'keeping the lights on'?	Be aware of the pitfalls of moving to a 'vanilla' SaaS system. The trade-off is a possible lack of flexibility in adapting or programming the system to meet your specific business needs. Understand, once again, what percentage of your existing IT time is spent on routine maintenance.
7.3 Is the primary determinant of considering Cloud to introduce new technologies and systems that will drive new value-added IT and business activities that are currently not possible in your organisation?	Do not exclude considering on-premises or traditionally hosted applications. Especially relevant for large systems such as ERP, where the total cost of ownership over a 5 year period, and increased flexibility of on-premises may indicate that Cloud is less suitable.
7.4 Is the primary determinant of considering Cloud to allow high risk innovation to occur due to the inherent flexibility of Cloud and low cost of a proof of concept (POC) trial?	Cloud is ideally suited to hi-risk innovation projects, however you are advised to perform a comprehensive due diligence before scaling up to production. Your Cloud costs could be a big surprise!
7.5 Is the primary determinant of considering Cloud to speed up IT system deployments?	Cloud may or may not be any quicker than on-premises, depending on your existing infrastructure. Do not assume that because it is Cloud it's quick. What percentage of elapsed time is spent outside of IT, waiting on business decisions etc? Good project governance and reporting should show this. The perceptions associated with 'slow' IT projects revolve around elapsed time, not total project hours. Know the difference and report it as such.

Question	Rationale
7.6 Is the primary determinant of considering Cloud to offer a way of simplifying the complexities of enterprise IT?	Cloud offers an additional layer of abstraction of the complexities of enterprise IT. If you need to integrate Cloud with any of your hosted or on-premises applications, you may not be able to avoid all of these complexities.
7.7 Is the primary determinant of considering Cloud to offer a way of putting IT systems in the hands of users?	The democratisation or consumerisation of IT is a common theme in Cloud. At the end of the day, which specific executive is accountable for the enterprise systems in your organisation?
7.8 Does your organisation's short term survival depend on the need to deploy systems at very short notice?	Cloud allows you to potentially deploy systems at short notice. If your organisation's short term survival depends on a Cloud system, you are unlikely to be too concerned about the long term costs, governance or risk issues.
7.9 Is the Cloud system providing a completely new system? (i.e. never existed before)	Moving to a clear system is a relatively simple exercise from a data entry perspective. HOWEVER, the design of the setup and configuration of the system could be complex and take some time. Get the system design right up front.

8. Governance

Question	Rationale
8.1 What undertakings does the provider give to ensure continued compliance to industry specific regulatory and statutory compliance standards, should they change at a future point in time?	If the Cloud provider is unwilling to modify their system to comply with a current or some future change in the regulatory mandates and standards in your jurisdiction, what recourse do you have under your contract to require them to make the necessary changes? (For example, Australian Prudential Regulation Authority, Draft Prudential Standard CPS 231, 'Outsourcing'). Worst case scenario, if you are operating non-compliant enterprise software systems you may be forced to change Cloud providers.
8.2 Which executive in your organisation has ultimate responsibility for technology and provider selection decisions?	Due to the transparent nature of Cloud computing, this allows all users to have an opinion on how, why where and when it could or should be implemented in your organisation! Accountability for the system should be assigned to the appropriate executive in your organisation.
8.3 Which executive has ultimate responsibility for the successful uptake of the Cloud technology? (i.e. realising the value)	Depending on the management structures in your organisation, this may be the project management office, line of business managers, or IT. What are the criteria for a 'successful' implementation, and how are these measured? The answer to this will depend on the scope and nature of the specific implementation in your organisation. Because the system is 'Cloud' is no guarantee of a successful implementation!

Question	Rationale
8.4 Will you need to retrieve its data on demand at any time from the Cloud?	You should have full title over your data resident in the provider's Cloud, and you should be able to retrieve it (i.e. export) at any time of your choosing in a suitable format, and without notice.
8.5 Do you have a consistent approach to Cloud computing in your organisation? Is IT centralised or federated across the various divisions or Business Units?	If your various Business Units are taking differing approaches to the implementation of Cloud computing under a federated IT governance management structure, will this cause you any problems if you wish to share data between divisions or at the enterprise level at a later date?
8.6 Due to the low entry cost and relative ease of access to Cloud technologies, would your organisation be concerned with the unmanaged proliferation of Cloud technologies?	Some organisations have already experienced the uncontrolled growth of Cloud computing across their organisations without appropriate governance. In which parts of your organisation will you allow this to occur, if at all?
8.7 Was the 'product demonstration' a key influential in your organisation decision to move to Cloud?	Reliance predominantly on a product demonstration is a high risk strategy for enterprise Cloud, as most of the risk, governance and cost issues are not clearly understood by the end users.

Question	Rationale
8.8 Has the Cloud provider bypassed IT (and targeted the senior non-IT executives, and line-of-business influential stakeholders) and adopted a 'Top-down' sales strategy?	Any attempt to bypass IT in the selection, governance and implementation of enterprise Cloud computing needs to be fully investigated. This relates to the core issue of accountability for the implementation of Cloud in your organisation. The benefits of Cloud computing can be democratised, however the cost, risk and governance cannot. Develop and implement a provider management policy on Cloud computing, which should form part of the Enterprise Cloud Computing Policy. This underpins good enterprise governance.
8.9 Is there a groundswell of enthusiasm for a Cloud solution by Non-IT Executives and users?	This is an enterprise and IT Governance / communications issue. The benefits of Cloud computing can be democratised, however the cost, risk and governance cannot. Develop and implement a provider management policy on Cloud computing. This should form part of the Enterprise Cloud Computing Policy and is core to good governance.
8.10 Is the ownership structure of the Cloud provider of concern to your organisation (private, joint venture, VC, or may have an obscure and opaque ownership structure)?	For important Cloud systems, the assessment of the credentials and financial viability of the provider is an important part of standard pre-purchase due diligence processes.

Question	Rationale
8.11 Who has title over your organisation's intellectual property that is vested in data schemas, business logic and/or programs that your organisation has written in the provider's infrastructure?	Can these programs be re-deployed to other clients, without your organisation approval, to the benefit of the provider or any other party? Can this be extracted at contract termination, and is so, in what form?
8.12 What is the life expectancy of the system?	If you run your subscription based Cloud system for a long period of time, it may be more cost effective to own and depreciate an equivalent system. Can you prove this or not? Know your cost exposure - in detail.
8.13 For multinationals: Does your local Cloud instance need to be configured differently to your Parent company's systems, and if so, what are the implications?	Sometimes, parent organisations mandate certain standard system configurations, data structures and formats that may not meet your local commercial, regulatory or statutory environment. How will you address these issues?
8.14 What security standards apply to the provider's infrastructure, and more importantly, are these standards of relevance to your organisation?	Identify what industry security, quality, operational and other standards apply to the provider's systems, environment and processes. Your customers may seek similar assurances from you if they depend on you and your systems to run their business.

Question	Rationale
8.15 Do you have a Cloud computing policy?	A Cloud computing policy is an important part of effective enterprise governance. Even if you are not intending to implement Cloud computing, you should nevertheless implement a policy to that effect.

9. Implementation

Question	Rationale
9.1 Will your organisation need to re-design and change your internal business processes to use the new Cloud system?	Changing the IT system is one thing, however, the costs of training line-of-business staff and managers in the use of the new system not to mention the updating of any procedural documentation should not be excluded from the overall project cost and effort.
9.2 Has your organisation clearly identified all the (including non-IT) staff costs and internal effort associated with data migration to the Cloud?	Changing technologies will require some changes in your business processes and procedures. How are you planning to manage and implement these changes across your organisation?
9.3 Is the user training on the new system likely to be very onerous?	End users will be presented with a new system. How are you planning to ensure that they all are proficient in its use and understand HOW the system is to be used? Training may also need to be provided across differing platforms. (e.g. PCs and Smartphone's)

Question	Rationale
9.4 Is the training effort for the new system a large effort for either the users or the administrators?	The ongoing management of the Cloud system will normally require a system administrator. This ensures system integrity, version control management and so on. Unless you are implementing a simple self-managing system, the training effort for the administrator(s) may not be trivial.
9.5 What IT staff re-training or restructuring needs to occur in switching to the Cloud?	Moving to the Cloud will most likely require a change in the skill sets in the IT department. What is the cost of releasing, or re-training staff?
9.6 Are there any costs associated with the data migration and conversion to get your organisation's data into (or from) other systems into the Cloud?	If data needs to me manipulated and transformed into the new system's formats, can you do this with any of the Cloud provider's current tools, or do you have to write conversion programs to do this? Third party Cloud integration tools may be available; however you need to validate the capability, cost and complexity of using these systems.
9.7 What is the mechanism by which your organisation can seamlessly convert your existing system and data to the Cloud? (If needed)	If you are migrating an existing system to the Cloud, what are the processes involved in moving your data to the Cloud? For enterprise applications such as ERP, CRM, content management, the data is unlikely to perfectly match the format of the providers system, and there may be missing meta-data, which would need to be manually or programmatically manipulated. Not a trivial exercise, depending on your specific implementation. Have you factored these costs into your business case?

Question	Rationale
9.8 Will your organisation need to segregate (Quality Of Service) Cloud traffic across your internal networks to maximise performance?	If the majority of your intra-company network traffic becomes Internet traffic, the networks may need to be reconfigured to allow this to occur without any degradation in performance. This may require an investment in additional bandwidth or a reconfiguration of the existing networks or both. Depending on the extent of your network infrastructure, this cost may not be trivial.

10. Innovation

Question	Rationale
10.1 Prototyping: Are you looking to start small then scale up if the proof of concept (POC) trial / prototype works?	Cloud systems can be very useful in supporting innovation initiatives, as they are low cost, flexible, with minimal walk away costs for small implementations. Whilst Cloud offers rapid scalability, you need to know what limits (processor, bandwidth, and data size or performance response times) apply in your provider's infrastructure.
10.2 Are you treating this system as a proof of concept (POC) 'trial' to foster innovation?	If a trial is a success do you know the total costs, effort and risks associated with a full scale-up up to production? Factor these into your business case.

11. Integration

Question	Rationale
11.1 Is the Cloud system standalone? (i.e. requires no interface to any other system)	A standalone Cloud system is possibly the quickest and easiest to implement, and is for this reason alone that the Small and Medium enterprise (SME) and consumer markets have such a high adoption and successful use of Cloud computing. Enterprise environments are somewhat different.
11.2 Will you be able to have competing Cloud providers collaborate on your enterprise projects?	If so, how can you assure this collaboration on large projects? You may need to manage a project that involved multiple vendors. Will your respective non-disclosure agreements inhibit effective multi-party collaboration on *your* project?
11.3 Is the incoming Cloud system replacing an existing system?	If you are transferring all application logic and data from your existing IT systems to the Cloud, the business logic and data migration effort can be significant, depending on the degree of complexity and your particular governance requirements. Scope this part of the migration project carefully, and test your assumptions on a limited *technical* proof of concept (POC) trial.

Question	Rationale
11.4 Will Cloud upgrades force you to upgrade anything on your IT infrastructure?	If the Cloud is connected to other systems, each time it is upgraded, it has the potential to disrupt the interfaces to other systems. This need to be reconfigured, tested and verified each time a system is upgraded. These may not occur at a time of your choosing. What is your position on this?
11.5 Does the lack of industry wide common system interchange standards for changing Cloud providers concern your organisation?	Whilst there may be no universal, common interchange standards between Cloud providers, there are likely third party applications that could fill this need. They may deliver the required functionality and capability in some respects, however have the potential to add cost and complexity.
11.6 Do you have rollback provision (technically) in case a migration or upgrade hits an unresolved obstacle?	If you have interface programs between the Cloud applications and your other systems, it is normal practice to have a pre-upgrade backup / restore point in the event the upgrade fails, for whatever reason. If your Cloud provider is unable to provide your restored data in a timely manner, this is a significant change control risk. This is not an issue if your Cloud instance is standalone. What is your position on this?

Question	Rationale
11.7 Will you need to include a new Cloud system under your 'single sign-on' regime?	You may need to purchase a third party single sign-on 'brokerage' application if no standard interfaces exist on your chosen Cloud system or existing IT infrastructure. This adds cost, complexity and possibly ongoing operational maintenance overhead associated in maintaining the cross reference relationships.
11.8 Will you need to exchange data between the Cloud and multiple other systems?	The more systems you have, the inter-system linkages can grow exponentially in number. This introduces added complexity, risk and cost. Modifying one system may require the modification of all the interfaces to that system. How do you intend to manage this?
11.9 Do you need to build any system interfaces between Cloud and your other IT systems, or can these be purchased 'off the shelf'?	Either building or purchasing system-system interfaces generally requires specific IT technical skills to implement and maintain, as it needs a detailed understanding of the underlying data structures and interface methods. Consultants may not understand *your existing system's data structures*, which implies that you are still somewhat reliant on your internal IT department's (or existing service provider's) involvement.

12. IT Staff

Question	Rationale
12.1 Are there any critical IT staff dependencies *during* the migration?	In large and/or complex Cloud implementations, you normally need to keep outgoing systems operating whilst the new system is being configured and tested. How will you manage the transitional staffing issues? (especially if key IT staff are to be made redundant on the completion of the migration project)
12.2 Internal IT: What staffing structures will your IT department require to support the ongoing operation of the Cloud system?	If you are retaining your existing systems, you may need to re-train existing IT staff (or re-contract your service provider). Is your IT staffing strategy clearly defined and costed?
12.3 Outsourced IT: Will your existing provider(s) be able to support the ongoing operation of the Cloud system?	What will occur if (i) your existing outsources provider(s) are direct competitor organisations to your Cloud provider, and/or (ii) they neither have the skill or capability to support the ongoing operation of your Cloud system? Moreover, if your Cloud provider (or their channel partners) do not offer outsourced operational services, does this mean that you have to introduce, yet another provider into the mix?

13. Contracts

Question	Rationale
13.1 Do you have an all encompassing, fully encapsulated contract with your Cloud provider that cannot change for the intended contract period?	Will a logon 'I accept' checkbox or anything on the provider's website extinguish, or dilute parts of your contract. If you order new licenses, will these be subject to the existing contract or an online contract at the time of purchase?
13.2 Are you aware of any legal precedence's in Cloud computing that relates to your (existing or potential) providers, and in your industry?	Make yourself aware of any relevant legal rulings relating to the use of Cloud technologies. This will help crystallise the known commercial and governance risks as experienced by other organisations in the adoption of Cloud technologies.
13.3 Are you able to negotiate contract variations?	As Cloud Computing is usually treated as a 'commodity' or standardised system, Cloud contracts are usually standard, and cannot be changed. Test the waters. If you have sufficient buying influence, contracts may be able to be modified in your favour.
13.4 Is your contract enforceable in a foreign legal jurisdiction?	Understand the legal jurisdiction(s) in which any remedies or actions are enforceable.
13.5 Are you aware of the potential costs and timelines of seeking remedies for major, persistent and material breaches by your provider under your agreement?	The costs and effort associated with seeking damages or mounting an action against your provider may be prohibitive.

Question	Rationale
13.6 Are you aware or concerned about the data transmission encryption standards and methods used, and if so, what information does the contract contain in this regard?	If there are substandard transmission security standards in obscure aspects of the provider's infrastructure, how would you know this?
13.7 Should the ownership of the Cloud provider change, what protection does your existing contract offer?	If the Cloud service provider is sold, acquired by another organisation, what contract transition issues exist between the outgoing and incoming providers when your organisation existing contract is up for renewal? Are you able to negotiate a perpetual agreement that potentially protects your interests in such an event?
13.8 What warranties, and warranty exclusions or limitations apply to all services offered?	Elements of The Competition and Consumer Act 2010 (Australian Commonwealth), for example may be relevant. Some laws offer rights that cannot be excluded or exchanged. Be aware of the rights under the foreign legal jurisdiction (if appropriate).
13.9 What are the implications should the Cloud provider be acquired by your competitor?	Is there are possibility of a regulator being concerned about anti-trust or market collusion should this occur?
13.10 What part do the multiple parties in the Cloud application stack play in the provider's contract?	Your provider may be using a range of third parties (possibly in foreign jurisdictions) to maintain and/or operate their systems and infrastructure. Are these relevant and/or covered in the contract?

Question	Rationale
13.11 What are the contract renewal terms in your Cloud provider's agreement(s)?	Contract renewal clauses may include automatic renewal, which may or may not be in your best interests.
13.12 What recourse do you have for non-performance penalties under your contracts?	Are service levels and the financial penalties for non-performance explicitly stated and measurable?
13.13 If offered, are subscription credits adequate compensation to your organisation in the event of a material non-performance by the Cloud provider?	If you are unable to run your business for 24-48 hours, for example, will the $20,000 subscription credits afforded to you under the contract be material when compared to your actual loss or cost?

14. Legislation

Question	Rationale
14.1 How can you access the system after contract end, to meet compliance requirements in terms of record retention?	Data may need to be accessed for a defined period (e.g. 10 years) either by legislation, or possibly as a result of litigation. Are you able to interpret the data in the event of a request for information? (You may have no programs with which to manipulate the data, as these have been left behind in the Cloud).
14.1 Which statutory and regulatory requirements apply to your organisation's IT systems and processes? What do these say about public Cloud?	You may be subject to a range of legislative, regulatory and other frameworks. You need to be aware of these obligations under the relevant frameworks irrespective of which IT systems are used.

14.2 Is the information retained in the Cloud subject to privacy legislation?	In Australia, National Privacy Principles (NPPs) may apply under the Privacy Act 1988 (Australian Commonwealth), or other equivalent laws under differing jurisdictions.
14.3 What are your organisation's document and information retention requirements for information held in the Cloud?	Your data may be subject to minimum retention periods under relevant Federal or State laws (e.g. Corporations Act 2001 (Australian Commonwealth), or other equivalent laws, depending on the relevant jurisdictions). How will you be able to access these documents if they are in electronic form, after you have left the Cloud provider? You may have the low level data but possibly not the software with which to recreate invoices, contracts, salary records, etc.

15. Multinational

Question	Rationale
15.1 International jurisdictions: Do you have any compelling mandate / need to retain on-premises, or in-country IT infrastructure?	Understand if there are any specific corporate, legislative or regulatory mandates as they apply to the system(s) in question. (e.g. if you are a government agency, or one of your customers is a government agency). This may have a bearing on your Cloud decisions, which may override any cost or efficiency considerations that are driving your plans to move to the Cloud.

Question	Rationale
15.2 Multinationals: Are you subject to the terms and conditions of a master contract set by your (overseas) parent company?	Check for the existence of any global agreements to eliminate the possibility of conflicting contracts, or parent company policy breaches.
15.3 Are there any trans-border data transmission issues or risks?	If your data traverses multiple countries, is this a concern to you?
15.4 Where is your data and system located?	Would your organisation have any issues with your and/or your customer's data (and software programs) being located overseas or in foreign legal jurisdictions?
15.5 If a global Cloud computing policy exists, what implications will that policy have for your local organisation?	Are there any conflicts between the mandates of a global policy on Cloud computing and your requirements? If so, what are they and are they a problem? Can you request changes to the global policy or seek exemptions if needed?
15.6 Which legal jurisdictions is the Cloud application subject to?	If all or parts of the provider's systems are resident overseas, international legal considerations apply. This may include all data mirrors, backup and secondary sites.
15.7 What statutory rights do foreign (or local) regulatory and security agencies have to demand access to your Cloud provider's system?	If your provider is served with a seizure warrant by statutory authorities, what are the implications for your organisation?

Question	Rationale
15.8 Does your Global policy mandate the use of a foreign resident SaaS system to ensure consistency of global standards?	If your organisation's customers (or future customers) include government or commercial organisations that preclude your organisation (contractually or by law) from allowing any of their information being resident on your organisation systems leaving the country, how would your organisation remedy this situation?
15.9 Has your overseas parent negotiated a global pricing deal with the Cloud provider(s)?	If your parent company has negotiated a global subscription pricing structure which does not include some specific services that your organisation wish to utilise, you may be charged full list price for these services if the provider understands that your unable to obtain competitive bids.

16. Procurement

Question	Rationale
16.1 Are you able to implement a tightly controlled technical pilot / proof of concept (POC) as part of the provider selection process?	As organisation's situations differ, the assumption that 'because it works somewhere else, it'll work here' may not necessarily be valid – and if it's quick to implement and easy to use – prove it.
16.2 Have you already attended the Cloud providers' demonstrations?	Be aware that undue reliance on the provider's product demonstration is insufficient evidence on which to make important decisions on your enterprise systems. Opinions as to the apparent fit for the system may ignore serious cost, risk and governance issues.

Question	Rationale
16.3 Does your provider offer either an unrestricted or enterprise type of Cloud offering?	Enterprise offerings may be offered and of some initial appeal to you. What minima apply to contract duration, number of users, etc.? What are the early termination penalty costs? Do you need to sign up for a multi year agreement? If so, why? After all it's supposed to be 'software as a service', the 'utility" computing model!
16.4 What is involved in switching between Cloud providers?	This is an important question, requiring a great deal of due diligence and careful project management. Core to the current Cloud model is a lack of a common interchange standard, which makes a switch to another provider not a trivial exercise. It is in essence, almost a full re-implementation.
16.5 Have you obtained a draft contract early on in the assessment process from each provider?	If your organisation is in the early / exploratory stages of a purchase can you get a copy of the standard contract? There may be some legal, governance, risk or performance problems in the contract itself. Better to know these early on.
16.5 Will the Cloud provider be delivering the full suite of implementation and support services?	Confirm which provider is delivering which services. Some SaaS Cloud providers do not provide the full suite of support services, and depend on their business partner channel. Will you need to perform a separate a due diligence on each supplier?

Question	Rationale
16.6 Can your organisation scale up and down use of Cloud services? If so are there minima?	Are you invoiced for what you have used on a monthly basis? Or are you billed annually in advance of what you might use? What mechanisms exist for you to recover costs for under usage?
16.7 What is the precise basis for invoicing and billing by the provider?	Invoicing models could take a variety of forms including peak usage in arrears, a per log-in event charge or prepaid expected usage. Are there any over usage or over quota penalties? Is any under-utilisation credited in arrears, if at all?. What is the Invoice frequency? Monthly or annually?

17. Risk & Security

Question	Rationale
17.1 Do you have a high dependency on IT systems?	If your organisation depends exclusively on your IT systems for its very existence, you need to be meticulous in your due diligence in moving to the Cloud.
17.2 Are there potential foreign exchange losses (or gains) if the Cloud provider requires billing in a foreign currency?	Can you have the system's costs invoiced in your local currency to ensure cost certainty?
17.3 Where, physically, is your data located?	Depending on your organisation, industry and/or prevailing statutory requirements, you may want to identify where your data is located. Your provider may be unwilling to disclose this, citing security considerations.

Question	Rationale
17.4 Can you get your data back easily and on demand at any time – If so, is this done with no involvement from the provider?	What are the specific processes by which you can extract all your data, and how long will this process take? How can you ensure that the data is a 'snapshot' of the entire system at a point in time? This is important from a data integrity point of view to ensure no transactions are lost.
17.5 Which third parties and individuals can access your data in the Cloud?	Your provider may not be willing to disclose this information, citing privacy or security reasons. Is this important to you?
17.6 Due to the hierarchical nature of most IT security systems, there usually needs to be a master administrator. Who has the top-level privileges in the Cloud Environment? How is this protected?	Some Cloud systems segment the master administrator from your data, and you are the only person who can see your data. Check how your specific provider's security is configured, implemented and managed.
17.7 What happens if the Cloud provider goes out of business?	This is one of the most commonly discussed questions. An obvious concern, and the response will depend on your specific provider's backup and escrow arrangements (if feasible).
17.8 Can you implement a Cloud Escrow arrangement in case the provider folds?	This issue required specific due diligence. It depends on the technical architecture of your provider. A truly multi-tenanted infrastructure most likely will not allow you to extract your specific system in its entirety so that it can be run elsewhere.

Question	Rationale
17.9 Are you concerned about provider lock-in?	The time, cost and effort of shifting to another provider at some point in the future is not trivial. Be aware of the risks associated with provider lock-in. Whilst your provider relationship may start off harmoniously, this could turn adversarial at some point, and the costs and effort of switching providers could present a challenge. Also, you are unlikely to be able to take advantage of very compelling competitor's offers, if the switch costs and effort is significant.
17.10 Does the provider have a disaster recovery plan and what scenarios does it cover?	Do not assume that because it's 'Cloud' you need not worry about Disaster Recovery. Other than natural disasters that may impact the provider's data centres and infrastructure, do not preclude the effects of a logical 'disaster', such as a shutdown or seizure by the regulatory authorities in the country of operation for whatever reason.
17.11 What happens if you do not want to take the software upgrade that the provider's about to implement?	How are software upgrades managed, and what are the change control processes that are applicable to your organisation? Are you forced to take each upgrade?

Question	Rationale
17.12 If you need to manage Cloud systems in conjunction with your on-premises systems, how does the software upgrade process work so that nothing breaks each time the Cloud provider upgrade their system?.	If your Cloud system has multiple interfaces to other systems, each time there is a Cloud system upgrade, you presumably need to test these inter-system interfaces. How can you do this if you have to just take what is given, and not at a time of your choosing? What are the governance and change control implications? For each upgrade, do you need to update any business processes, user documentation, etc.?
17.13 How do you convert your data from the old Cloud to the new Cloud (or other system)?	Unless your new system has already got the specific data converters with which to read and manipulate the data into the format that it can use, you will either need to write programs to do this, or purchase a third party system that allows you do this transformation without programming effort. This may, nevertheless, not be a trivial exercise.
17.14 Do all your users have reliable access to high-speed, low latency Internet?	Cloud depends on the Internet exclusively. If there are reliability or speed problems, this may be a problem for those affected.
17.15 What staff and contractor security vetting and related governance processes exist in the vendor's environment?	Sometimes, the greatest threat to the integrity of a system is the human element. The damage that a disgruntled or ill-trained, accident prone employee or contractor could be significant. What *systemic* controls exist in the vendor's environment to mitigate this exposure, and how often are these controls independently tested?

Question	Rationale
17.16 Can you access the relevant system logs that indicate any low level administrative activities which have occurred in *your instance* of the Cloud environment?	Depending on your security position and risk appetite, you may wish to view the various underlying system administration and other low level logs that relate to *your instance* of the Cloud environment. If you needed to do this, how could it be done? This would include such information such as system administration 'back-door' access to your environment.
17.17 What forensic capability does the Cloud provider's environment offer?	In extreme cases, a forensic analysis of the vendor's infrastructure or databases may be required. How could this be achieved?

18. Service Level Agreements + Penalties

Question	Rationale
18.1 What are the loss or service credit limitation provisions under the contract in the event of non-performance or system outages?	In certain instances, the credit offered in lieu of performance shortfalls, may be trivial compared to the actual loss incurred by your organisation. What is your position on this?
18.2 How is system availability and performance measured and reported?	What are the specific definitions of an 'outage' or system failure? Are any service credits defined on a per incident basis or cumulative over a defined period (e.g. month)? If your organisation Cloud provider measures and offers compensation on a non-availability per event basis up to a defined time period (e.g. 10 minutes per event), how would your organisation seek compensation should multiple and persistent (e.g. 9 minute outage) events occur below this threshold?

18.3 What Service Level Agreement / Service Availability standards are written into the contract?	Service levels should be specified in the Contract, and not referred to in general terms. Are planned maintenance outages included or excluded from any calculations?
18.4 Will you need to change / implement any performance monitoring systems to measure the service levels of the Cloud?	How will you be able to verify the performance claims made by your provider? (Assuming that it's very important to your organisation).

19. Third Party Applications

Question	Rationale
19.1 Are you fully aware of the legal and governance issues relating to third party software run on the Cloud provider's infrastructure that you may elect to use?	Depending on the provider, third parties may be able to write custom applications on the Cloud provider's infrastructure that complies with the provider's minimum technical and performance standards. This allows these third parties to run an independent business, selling and supporting their own applications in the Cloud. You may be purchasing these applications from the third party providers under a separate agreement to your provider's main agreement. These applications may be completely standalone, or act as an extension to the Cloud provider's core systems.

Question	Rationale
19.2 What is your position should third party application provider(s) (that have developed applications on the Cloud provider's infrastructure) cease to exist?	Confirm what, if any, service continuity guarantees are offered by your Cloud provider for these third party applications. Can you seek assurances that these applications will remain active for long enough for you to seek alternative suppliers.
19.3 What obligations exist for the Cloud provider to assure the quality, security, integrity and performance of the third party applications hosted on their infrastructure?	Third parties can write applications on the Cloud provider's infrastructure that comply with the provider's minimum technical and performance standards and are certified as such. The Cloud provider may not warrant these applications in any way, and you will be accepting the third parties' terms as-is. As such, they may present an unacceptable risk, present governance or other problems. Each of these third party agreements should be subject to their own due diligence assessment.
19.4 Are you fully aware of the costs associated with any third party applications that are run on the provider's infrastructure?	Do you purchase these from the third party providers directly under a separate purchase agreement?
19.5 Have you factored in the additional costs of purchasing, installing and maintaining any additional 'plug-in' or third party software?	Often a Cloud system's capabilities are enhanced with a range of third party software items that are written to run on the Cloud provider's infrastructure. The cost of these, both in terms of subscription, ongoing support and maintenance may not be trivial. Additionally, will your Cloud provider levy any additional charges for the use of these applications across all devices (e.g. Smart phones, PCs, laptops)

Index

Accountability, xv, 15, 16, 24, 140, 142
> Federated structure, 39, 40
> Stakeholder , 123-125
> System integrity, 38

Assessment Framework, xxiv, 117, 118-120

Brand damage, 87

Cloud computing:
> Analogy (Electricity grid), xiv, 17, 88-89, 91
> Awareness of, 1
> Compelling nature of, xv, 2, 9-10, 11-12, 22, 15, 142
> Definition of, 3
> Elements of, 4, 5, 6
> Enthusiasm for, 7, 9, 32, 37, 43, 142
> Low barrier to entry, 25
> Maturity of, xiv, 90
> Potential of, 11
> Vendor lock-in: See Vendor

Configuration, 32, 89, 96, 99, 108, 139, 143
> Vs. Programming, 19

Consumerisation (of IT): See Democratisation (of IT)

Contract, 9-10, 41, 73, 120, 140
> Considerations, xxii, 41-50
> Duration, 42, 43
> Enterprise, 73
> Master, 155
> Penalties, 46-47, 153, 162
> Termination (transition out) , 10, 81, 131–133, 136, 143, 153

Compliance
> Statutory / Regulatory, 47, 109, 140

Cost
> Apps, and plug-ins, 71
> Break-even, 64, 65
> Foreign exchange gains/losses, 72
> Implementation, 75
> Per user per month per application: See PUPMA
> Project, 144
> Total Cost of Ownership (TCO), xxiv, 10, 25, 60, 64, 71, 75, 103, 106, 113, 135, 138
> Vendor switching costs, 73, 87

Democratisation (of IT), xxi, 11, 17, 139

Disaster Recovery, 15, 80, 160

Enterprise systems, 12, 18, 21, 22, 28, 33, 99
  Accountability over, 24
  CRM, 5, 8, 20, 67, 145
  ERP, 8, 18, 138, 145
  Life expectancy, 103
  Proprietary, 100
  Unauthorised, 23, 25

Escrow, 1, 79, 84, 90, 159

Executive management
  Accountability, 1, 3, 15, 24, 39, 139, 140
  Frustration with IT, 21, 40
  'Top-down' vendor sale, 37-39, 142

Governance, xiii, 1, 6, 9, 10, 32
  Accountability for, 15, 24
  Organisation scale, xvi, 23

Hype-Cycle, 6- 8

IaaS (Infrastructure as a Service), 5-6

Innovation, 32, 33, 138

Insurance, 84

Integration, 29 -33, 53, 120-121, 130, 145, 147

Intellectual property, 48, 143

Interfaces (system): See Integration

Internet, 3, 5, 13, 77, 96, 97, 146, 161

IT Department
  Cloud transforming, 21-22
  Wedge between business, 37

Legal, 2, 41-50, 93, 108, 131, 151-154, 157, 163
  Jurisdiction, 2, 10, 48, 93, 155
  Patriot Act (USA), 78

License (software), 61-63, 105, 134, 136
  Concurrent usage model, 61-63
  Named user model, 61, 63
  Server based, 61-63

Multinational, xvi, 25, 45, 82, 93-97

Multi-tenanted, 2, 6, 13-14, 137

On-premises, xv- xvii, 16-18, 24, 31, 33, 35, 60

Outsourcing, 2, 9, 10, 140

PaaS (Platform as a Service), 5, 6

Performance, 9, 74, 146
  Degradation, 63
  Limits, xvii, 74
  Monitoring, 163

Index

Networks, 146

Third party apps, 163-164

Policy

Absence of, 25, 81

Cloud, xvii, 40, 144

Conflicts, 97

Global, 45

Governance, 109

Procurement, 24, 142

Settings, 94-95

Private Cloud, xvi, 13, 14, 16, 109

Procurement, xxi, 16, 26, 40, 43, 117, 156

Bypassing IT, 81

Implications, 23

Policy, 24

Programming: (*See* Configuration)

Project xiii, xv, 18, 21, 26, 27, 28, 31, 144

Governance, 138

Issues, 109-112

IT Staff dependencies, 74

Large (enterprise), 18, 147

Migration, 147, 150

Multi-party collaboration, 147

On-premises, 18

Pilot, *see* Proof of Concept

Prince2 / PMBOK, 108

Speed and Cloud, xv, 21,

Start-up, 36

Stressed Cloud projects, xvii

Proof of Concept, xxii, 52, 53, 57, 105, 137-138, 146-147, 156

Public Cloud: xiii, xvi, 2, 3, 10, 13, 14, 16, 20, 21, 28, 100, 109, 153

PUPMA, 66, 70 135, *See also* Cost

Risk xiii-xvi, xxi, xxiii, 2, 6, 11, 15-16, 115, 117

Appetite, 113, 128

Foreign exchange, 134

In pilot projects, 32

Runaway complexity, 29

SaaS, xiii, 6

Scale-up, xvi, 32

Third party apps, 35

Viral cloud, 23-25

SaaS (Software as a Service), xiii, 2, 5, 6, 10-11, 16, 19, 24, 42, 43, 45, 51, 65, 82

Scale-down, 43, 104

Scale-up, xvi, 20, 25, 32, 33, 43, 60, 110, 111, 146, 158

Software subscription: *See* License

SOX / JSOX, 2, 108

Staff, 72, 74, 102, 120, 144, 145, 150

Third party, 20, 35, 111, 134, 145, 148, 149, 161, 163, 164

Total Cost of Ownership (TCO) *see* Cost

User types (in Cloud), 49, 74, 75, 82, 134, 136

Utility computing, xiii - xv, xxi, xxiii, 17, 88, 90–91, 157

Vendor, xiv, xxii

Lock-in, 25, 73, 91, 132, 133, 160

Switching to new, 87

Bypassing IT, 12

'Top-down' selling approach, 37

Pet-shop marketing, 36

Viral Cloud, 24-25, 81, 82, 84